The Great American Chocolate Chip Cookie Book

The Great American Chocolate Chip Cookie Book

Carolyn Wyman

The Countryman Press
Woodstock, Vermont

Book design and composition by Vicky Vaughn Shea, Ponderosa Pine Design

Library of Congress Cataloging-in-Publication Data
Wyman, Carolyn.
The great American chocolate chip cookie book / Carolyn Wyman. -- First edition.
pages cm
Includes bibliographical references and index.
ISBN 978-1-58157-162-2 (pbk. : alk. paper)
1. Chocolate chip cookies. I. Title.

TX772.W94 2013
641.86'54--dc23

2013028201

The Great American Chocolate Chip Cookie Book
978-1-58157-162-2

Published by The Countryman Press, P.O. Box 748, Woodstock, VT 05091
Distributed by W. W. Norton & Company, Inc., 500 Fifth Avenue, New York, NY 10110
Printed in the United States of America

10 9 8 7 6 5 4 3 2 1

Permissions and Credits
All text and photos by Carolyn Wyman except for the following photographs or specified illustrations, text, recipes, and trademarks for which grateful acknowledgment is made. Courtesy Nestlé: 6, 8 middle, 10 left, 24 bottom right, 31, 33 left and right, 59 bottom right, 65, 73, 86, 92 photo and recipe, 122, 123 photo and recipe, 137 recipe, 139 photo and recipe, 156 photo and recipe, 158 recipe, 159 illustration, 170. NESTLÉ® and TOLL HOUSE® are registered trademarks of Societe des Produits Nestlé S.A., Vevey, Switzerland, and are used with permission.; p. 8 bottom: Doonesbury © 1970 G. B. Trudeau. Reprinted with permission of Universal Uclick. All rights reserved; p. 10: Chips Ahoy is a registered trademark of Kraft Foods Global Brands. Otis Spunkmeyer is a registered trademark of Aryzta LLC. McDonald's is a registered trademark of McDonald's Corp. p. 11: Famous Amos is a registered trademark of the Famous Amos Chocolate Chip Cookie Co.; Stonehill College Archives and Historical Collections/Stanley A. Bauman Photograph Collection: 19, 20, 21 left, 24 middle, 36; Carol Goldman: 1, 11 top, 118; Kathleen King/Tate's Bake Shop: 10 bottom right and 85 bottom left (photos

Permissions and Credits continue on page 193

For James "Dad" Wyman, the block off which
I am the grateful (nonchocolate) chip

HIS ONE WEAKNESS–
. . . Toll House Cookies from home. Now that Nestle's Semi-Sweet Chocolate is harder to get—because so much of it is going to the fighting forces in emergency and combat rations—put it to the best possible use. Make up a batch of those golden-brown, crunchy Toll House Cookies and send it to that soldier boy of yours. He always did go for those crisp, brown cookies containing whole pieces of Nestle's Semi-Sweet Chocolate. You'll find the easy-to-make recipe on every package.
When your dealer is temporarily out of Nestle's Chocolate products, please be patient. Remember the demands of our armed forces are heavy, but they must come first.
NESTLÉ
SEMI-SWEET CHOCOLATE
BACK THE ATTACK WITH WAR BONDS

Contents

Introduction

I've eaten more chocolate chip cookies in my lifetime than any other single food. Home-baked and store-bought, from fancy bakeries and modest bodegas, crispy and cakey, with coffee for breakfast and milk for dessert, I've hardly ever met a chocolate chip cookie I didn't like. It is my favorite food by far.

Nestlé® Original Toll House® Cookies

I'm not alone in this. I'm not even in the minority. Chocolate chip cookies are indisputably America's favorite, accounting for more than half of all cookies baked at home, 6 billion packaged cookies sold annually at U.S. supermarkets, and selling at four times the rate of any other cookie at the Cookie Studio in Atlanta, Georgia, and most other bakeries and cookie stores around the country. It's among only four foods acceptable to even the pickiest eaters (the other three are fried chicken, French fries, and macaroni and cheese), according to a 2002 University of Pennsylvania study (if you're looking for a sure hit for the next potluck). It's so popular that a defining statement of the profile *60 Minutes* did on the retirement of famous curmudgeon Andy Rooney was a clip of him saying, "You know one thing I don't like? Chocolate chip cookies."

Early Doonesbury strip that speaks to the universal appeal of this cookie

The chocolate chip's popularity has even spawned spin-off megahits like chocolate chip

ice cream sandwiches and chocolate chip cookie dough ice cream.

How to explain this?

The chocolate chip cookie is the perfect balance of sweet dough and rich chocolate. At least to Americans. Unlike the hamburger and Coca-Cola, chocolate chip cookies are one American food icon that can be hard to find elsewhere. That's why Japanese tourists put eating one high on their list of things to do in New York City, and why Nestlé® has yet to make the Toll House® morsel packaging bilingual (for fear the product would lose its cachet as a touchstone of American assimilation).

Like Americans themselves, the chocolate chip cookie is friendly, straightforward, and democratic: accessible to all at its many price levels and in its many forms. That the three businesspeople most associated with the cookie at the height of its retail sales success were a woman, a Jewish man, and an African American man (and that two of the three were of extremely modest beginnings) is testament to America at its melting-pot and land-of-opportunity best.

Chocolate chip cookies are also easy to make at home. It is, in fact, the first recipe many people ever attempt and the only thing many bake as adults. This tie to childhood—memories of making chocolate chip cookies with Mom or Mom making the cookies for you—is one big reason it's so beloved. It explains why even the most hardened adult instantly becomes a smiling kid upon being handed a warm one. It also probably explains how the just-referenced Wally Amos and Debbi Fields went on to successful careers as motivational speakers. As Debbi Fields once said, "I've never felt like I was in the cookie business. . . . My job is to sell joy. My job is to sell happiness."

Roasting Plant cookie

The chocolate chip cookie is also highly adaptable to added ingredients and tweaks—hence, why everyone thinks their chocolate chip cookie recipe is the best. In

Profile of a Fan

Who eats chocolate chip cookies? As might be expected, given their overall popularity, they're the first choice of men, women, and kids—although the largest volume of sales comes from families with kids.

Asked who buys Nestlé® Toll House® morsels, Nestlé executive Kelly Malley says, "Moms." Asked who buys the Nestlé Toll House cookie dough she says, "Moms who don't have as much time." On average, people bake with Toll House morsels three to four times a year, although it's more for Midwesterners and older folks, according to Nestlé Toll House marketing manager Susan Geringer. Packaged cookie mixes are popular with seniors who grew up with the baking habit but no longer bake often enough to want to keep separate baking ingredients on hand. Judging by sales data for cookies and chocolate chips, people eat 10 times as many packaged supermarket chocolate chip cookies (Chips Ahoy et al.) as from-scratch or baked from packaged dough (with from-scratch now just slightly edging out baked-off ones six to four). More than half of all chocolate chips end up in cookies, and the vast majority of all chocolate chips are sold at holiday time. In fact, Nestlé Toll House marketing director Jim Coyne says the company's morsels are typically among the top-selling items sold in supermarkets in the last eight weeks of the year.

Nestlé morsels advertisement

Kids like their chocolate chip cookies without nuts and crispy, although a soft cookie is preferred by adults and 74 percent of the general populace (at least according to not-exactly-impartial soft-cookie maker Otis Spunkmeyer).

Chocolate chip cookies are most often eaten between meals, though sometimes for dessert or before bed, according to a comprehensive study of chocolate chip cookie eating behavior commissioned by the now defunct Sunshine Biscuits (although naughty-food-habit king McDonald's sells more than 20 percent of its cookies at breakfast time). Most people eat them with milk. Coffee, ice cream, or hot chocolate are the next most popular accompaniments. Over 40 percent dunk their cookies before eating.

As for quantities: The majority of people eat two to four 2-inchers at a sitting. But 43 percent of American adults admit to at least once having downed 10 at a sitting, and an impressive 13.5 percent to having eaten 20 or more at a time (and not for a chocolate chip cookie–eating contest, either). If that sounds like you, are you ever reading the right book!

Tate's Bake Shop cookies

Carol's Cookies

fact, the biggest surprise for me in working on this book was the amazing diversity of cookies that can be produced from one basic recipe. "Just as France has its mother sauces, this is our mother cookie," food writer David Leites told me. This cookie has also changed with the times. In our collective lives, it has gone from upscale restaurant fare to homemade treat to supermarket staple to retail store craze, and back to high-end baked good again; in our individual lives, from after-school snack to girl bait to something to bake for your kids when they get home from school.

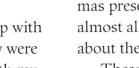

Toll House restaurant cookie tin

Like most Americans, I grew up with Nestlé® Toll House® cookies. They were a special rainy-day treat I made with my mom. Although my mother also baked brownies and quick breads, these were her only cookie. I think her feeling was, why bother with anything else when you have found perfection? Even now with my more expanded cookie horizons of sugar and oatmeal and peanut butter, I have to agree.

My dad grew up only one town over from the cookie's Toll House restaurant birthplace and both my parents dined there a number of times. My mother distinctly remembers scoring big points with my father's elderly grandmother at a lunch there where the waitress offered to cut the corn off the cob for her. Great Nana Wyman had apparently never before experienced such service or care in a restaurant.

Given that chocolate chip cookie pedigree, is it any wonder that the Famous Amos stand was stop one on my first trip to Los Angeles in 1976? Or that for years, new athletic socks stuffed with homemade chocolate chip cookies were my standard token Christmas present? Or that I have long owned almost all of the previous books written about the chocolate chip cookie?

These books have been mainly cookbooks, a few disappointingly featuring any food you can put chocolate chips in, rather than recipes showcasing the

Why Nestlé® Isn't Crying in Their Kleenex over Companies Xeroxing Their Toll House® Name

Like "thermos," "aspirin," "cellophane," and "shredded wheat," the term "Toll House cookie" is no longer a valid trademark, opined the *New York Times* and many other newspapers after Nestlé lost a $5 million trademark infringement suit they had brought against the owners of the Toll House restaurant in August 1983.

And yet the term "Toll House" is capitalized and called a registered trademark in all major current dictionaries. Why?

After the Saccone family bought the Toll House in 1973, they expanded sales of Toll House cookies to supermarkets in nearby states. Whereupon Nestlé filed suit, arguing that Ruth Wakefield had given them the exclusive right to sell cookies under the term *Toll House*.

Federal law allows for the cancellation of any trademark deemed to have become a common name. Arguing that Nestlé's own marketing surveys showed that "to most consumers, Toll House was associated with a type of product," and "not the product of a specific manufacturer," Federal Judge M. Joseph Blumenfeld ruled in favor of the Saccones—though even they had mixed feelings about the verdict.

In winning, "we lose too," Donald Saccone told a reporter at the time, because "the use of the word Toll House is now available to anyone," thus potentially opening up their Toll House cookie business to tractorfuls of new competition.

And so lawyers for both sides huddled and in spring 1985 came up with a secret settlement conditioned on getting Blumenfeld to vacate or cancel his prior trademark decision.

Blumenfeld went along, hence the ® symbol you see next to Toll House on this page and elsewhere in this Toll House cookie book.

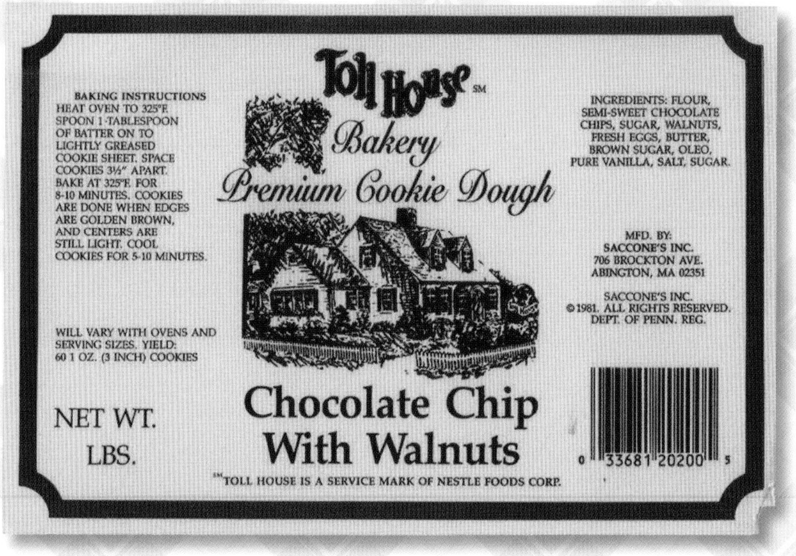

1980s' Saccone Toll House cookie dough label

cookie's distinctive brown-sugar-and-chocolate taste (the rule for this book). The few that talk about the history of the cookie at all restrict their comments to its invention. Yes, as obvious and ubiquitous as this cookie now is, it *was* invented only 75 years ago, though not in the accidental way that is served up by other chocolate chip cookie book authors and on the Internet. I, on the other hand, was able to talk to Ruth Wakefield's daughter and many of her former employees at the Toll House restaurant and scour historic documents to get the real story.

Famous 4th Street Cookies

I was also lucky enough to have been able to talk to past cookie giants Amos, Fields, and David Liederman, and present ones at Nestlé®, Tate's Bake Shop, and Levain Bakery and hear firsthand

Mixing dough for the world's biggest chocolate chip cookie

their really interesting stories—about Wally Amos's first career as a talent agent who discovered Simon and Garfunkel; the Nestlé® party catered by Martha Stewart featuring a 3,000-pound chocolate chip that had to be lifted into the New York City banquet facility by crane; and Kathleen's Cookies' dramatic rebirth as Tate's.

Arguably even better were all the chocolate chip cookies I got to taste while working on this book, both during recipe testing sessions and at a chocolate chip cookie potluck party I threw on my birthday in spring 2012. Some people who came to that party or who otherwise knew I was working on this book have since asked me, "Aren't you sick of chocolate chip cookies now?"

In a word, no (I type, half-eaten cookie at my keyboard's side). Working on this book has, on the contrary, opened my eyes to this cookie's amazing story and heightened my understanding and appreciation for all a chocolate chip cookie is and can be. Here's raising a tall, cold glass of milk that this book will do the same for you.

The author's chocolate chip cookie dessert-tasting party

1

Side Dish

The stock market had suffered its worst drop in U.S. history. Banks failed, stores and factories closed, leaving millions without work and many others homeless. In short, the country was suffering unprecedented misery, without the comfort of chocolate chip cookies.

Ruth Wakefield, circa 1940

It would not seem to be the best time to chuck a steady paycheck and live your dream of running your own restaurant as Ruth and Kenneth Wakefield did in Whitman, Massachusetts in late August 1930.

Toll House restaurant in 1930

"Ken and I would go out to eat from time to time and we'd usually be disappointed," Ruth explained to a reporter many years later. "We would question why you could never have soup without paying extra but you'd get a dessert you wouldn't want. They'd measure out little pats of butter and little things for cream." In short, they wanted to create the restaurant of their dreams.

Despite the couple's complementary sets of useful experiences (Ruth had taught home ec at a local high school and Kenneth was an executive with a meat-packing firm), and their conservative choice of a small tea room on a well-traveled former toll road (which inspired the restaurant's name), the Toll House was a risky venture for people just starting out. Fixing the building up and furnishing it left them with operating capital of only $50.

Their first customer was a local socialite who brought her women's club for lunch, which was a great success until she asked them to send her a check, leaving them with only $20. A lone couple of Pennsylvania tourists dined the second day, mainly because the man had lived in the house when he was a child. With only $10 left after buying more food, the Wakefields and their two employees sat around worrying for most of the third day, running to the window whenever they heard a car approach to see if it would stop.

The inn's iconic sign

When more than one of the seven tables were taken, salad plates from their limited supply of dishware would be whisked away from one table only to reappear a few moments later freshly washed and bearing dessert at another.

But by Christmas, the Wakefields needed a dozen employees to handle all the business; by the third year, four times that. By 1938, 100 employees served the 1,000 diners who daily filled the original building and the sprawling caterpillar of additions, including a room surrounding a live tree.

The Toll House's success was a consequence of not only its tasteful, homey décor and delicious food and its prime location on the main route between Boston and the Cape Cod summer vacation destination, but also the Wakefields' timing. As bad as the economy was, the rise of the automobile and the middle class launched many highly profitable eateries during the Depression. Harland Sanders'

The Toll House's success made it a near-permanent construction site, as this Wakefield holiday card acknowledged.

fried chicken shop is another example. And in New England from the late 1930s to the late 1960s, the Toll House was almost as renowned. As such it was a celebrity magnet (Cole Porter, Ethel Merman, the Astors, Joe DiMaggio, Betty Davis, Gloria Swanson, Eleanor Roosevelt, and Rocky Marciano all dined there) and a special-occasion place for locals who better appreciated the on-the-house seconds. That included lobster dishes, for which the Toll House was famous. They were among a large collection of traditional New England recipes Ruth had inherited from her grandmother and brought to the restaurant, along with her own creations, and adaptations of dishes the Wakefields tried on the overseas trips they took every January after the restaurant became successful. As legendary journalist Ernie Pyle said in his 1938 three-part profile about the place: "Ruth Wakefield can cook 'by ear.' Or by taste, I suppose you'd call it. She can taste a strange dish, and come home and recreate it with every ingredient in proportion."

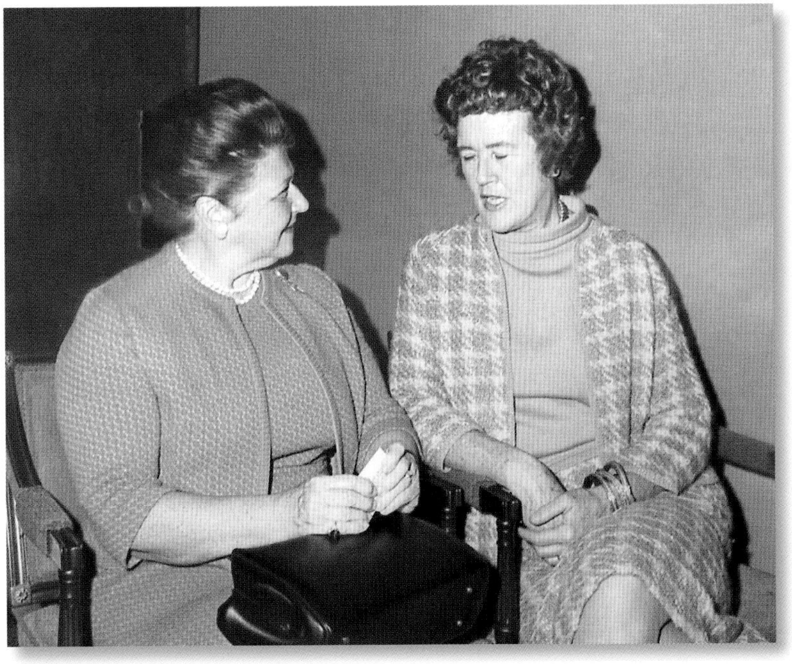

Ruth Wakefield and Julia Child

"Her curiosity on recipes is unbounded," echoed the jacket flap of Ruth's *Toll House Tried and True Recipes* cookbook, first published in 1931. "No interesting dish has been too difficult for her to track down in a Parisian restaurant or a South American café. She is also of the inventive turn herself, and it is her very own creations which have so delighted . . . her weekly guests." That book was reprinted 28 times before 1954, and grew like the restaurant; from a slim volume padded with stain removal tips and first-aid advice to an 888-recipe best-seller.

The restaurant was particularly famed for its desserts, which by the early 1940s had their own menu and numbered 15. Joseph Kennedy Sr. stopped there twice a week for years for a double wedge of their Boston cream pie and to have gingerbread and brownies sent to his kids (including future president John Kennedy, when he was with the Navy in the South Pacific). Famous early food critic (and later cake-mix maker) Duncan Hines rhapsodized about their three-inch-high lemon meringue pie, baba au rhum (rum-soaked cake), and Indian pudding, which the quotable Hines famously called "the kind of dessert that makes a fellow wish for hollow legs." A few butterscotch wafer cookies were routinely served on the side of a dish of ice cream, but they were not on the menu or mentioned by Hines or anyone else who wrote about the restaurant at the time.

The Toll House's food was rivaled only by its exceptional service. Especially in those early days, Ken and Ruth were almost always there to greet customers and oversee the operation. "Ruth had a genius for making guests feel welcome and comfortable," recalls former waitress June O'Leary. But with staff, "she could be demanding. She wanted perfection and she'd yell at people if she didn't get it," O'Leary remembers. Waitresses trained for three months before getting the full evening workload of two tables, which might not seem like much unless you know what was expected: silverware placed one thumbprint away from the edge of the table (or the entire table setting done over), orders memorized,

Ruth entertains Duncan Hines and company in the Toll House's Garden Room.

The ever-gracious hostess

uniforms "neatly pressed, stocking seams straight, shoes clean," as ordered by the restaurant's seven-page service manual.

"No military machine or factory production line was ever geared to more smooth-running cohesion," the restaurant's post-war promotional booklet rather grandiosely intoned. "Long-range planning and constantly studied personnel are reflected in an operating teamwork flawless in its unruffled perfection. Confusion is unknown."

In short, this is not the kind of place you would expect to run out of basic food supplies in the middle of evening service.

And yet the number-one most oft-repeated story about how and why Ruth Wakefield invented the chocolate chip cookie is that she ran out of nuts for a

If You Think Her Cookies Were Good . . .

If you'd previously heard of Ruth Wakefield at all, it's probably as the inventor of the chocolate chip cookie. But former employees and patrons of her Toll House restaurant seem to regard the cookies as among the least of her culinary creations: Her Indian pudding was on Duncan Hines's 1947 list of his 12 all-time favorite U.S. restaurant dishes. Her sticky bun–like butterscotch pecan biscuits were a bread-basket offering that at least three ex-employees said were as popular or more popular than the cookies. You can find these and many other Toll House recipes in any edition of Wakefield's *Toll House Tried and True Recipes* cookbook, including the 1940 public domain one at the Internet's Open Library (www.openlibrary.org).

Toll House dessert spread

cookie they served and, in a panic or a pinch, decided to substitute pieces of chocolate cut up from a bittersweet chocolate bar she had on hand. This story is all over the Internet and is also told by most of the restaurant's living ex-employees, with the exception of Carol Cavanagh, a former waitress and daughter of longtime Toll House grill man George Boucher. She repeats her late father's story about the day vibrations from a Hobart mixer caused some chocolate stored on a shelf to fall into a bowl of cookie dough in the Toll House kitchen. (Boucher becomes the hero of this tale by persuading Ruth Wakefield to try baking the cookies rather than following her initial inclination to throw them out.)

Toll House restaurant plate

Although Wakefield appeared on local radio cooking shows, talked to newspaper food editors and make public

How Did She Invent the Cookie? Let Us Count the Bogus Theories

Although the ran-out-of-nuts story is definitely the most popular, there are almost as many stories about how Ruth Wakefield invented the chocolate chip cookie as there are chocolate chip cookie recipes. Here are a few more of these testaments to the American creative imagination I heard in my quest for the real story (source names withheld to protect the guilty):

- She was trying to make chocolate-flavored cookies but was too lazy or pressed for time to melt the chocolate ahead of time, and thought the baking heat might do the trick.
- She had some pieces of chocolate left over from another recipe and, being frugal, decided to throw them into some nut cookie batter she was making.
- She didn't have enough butter to make her butter cookies and thought the cocoa butter in a chocolate bar might provide the needed extra fat.
- She ran out of nuts and chocolate but decided to try using a big chocolate bar she had gotten as a gift from Andrew Nestlé® (if there even was one, the Nestlés having sold the business more than half a century earlier).

appearances to promote her book and the restaurant in the 1930s and '40s, she was mainly mum on the subject of the cookie's invention. Wakefield merely teases future cookie scholars in the 1948 revision of her cookbook, the first to feature personal commentary, when she writes, "I suppose most of you know Toll House . . . Cookies. Their origin and development is really a story by itself"—which she then, infuriatingly, does not tell!

But Wakefield did talk about the cookie's invention to several reporters in the 1970s. "We had been serving a thin butterscotch nut cookie with ice cream. Everybody seemed to love it, but I was trying to give them something different. So I came up with the Toll House cookie," Wakefield told *Boston Herald-American* reporter Virginia Bohlin in 1974. Bohlin wrote that Wakefield "worked out the recipe on the way back from a trip to Egypt."

Several years later *Christian Science Monitor* reporter Phyllis Hanes similarly described how Wakefield took an ice pick to a Nestlé® semi-sweet chocolate bar "to add to some brown sugar dough at her Toll House Restaurant. She had been looking for an alternative to the crisp pecan icebox cookie she usually served with ice cream."

Indeed the very first edition of Wakefield's *Tried and True* cookbook contains a recipe for Nut Tea Wafers that sounds very much like the one these reporters described and also a lot like the Toll House® Chocolate Crunch Cookie—Wakefield's original name for Toll House cookies—that first appears in her cookbook in 1938 with white sugar and chocolate added. Butterscotch cookie recipes similar to Wakefield's Nut Tea Wafers also show up in other cookbooks of the era, including the 1936 edition of *Joy of Cooking*.

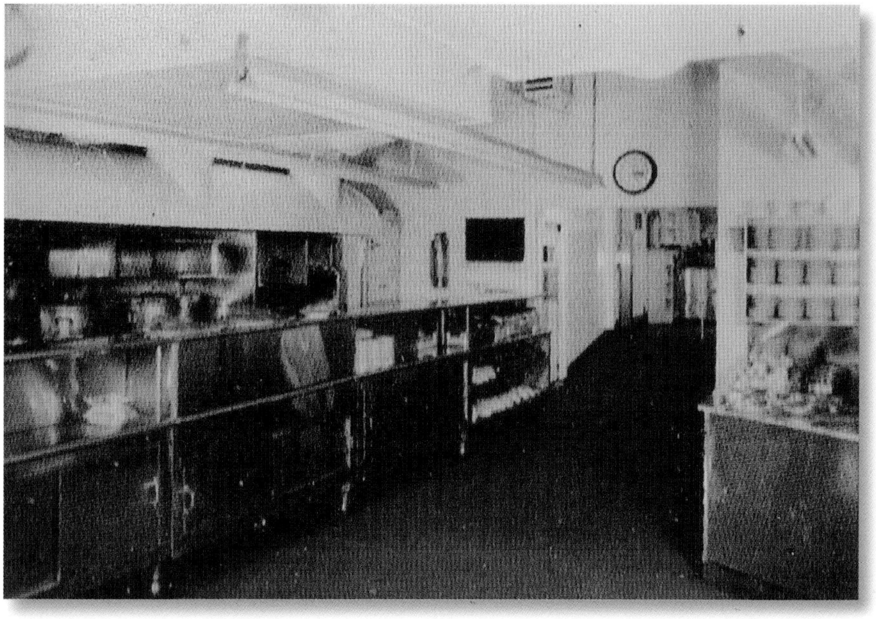

Toll House restaurant kitchen

Ruth's Original Toll House® Cookie Recipe (Toll House Chocolate Crunch Cookies)

Nestlé® made several changes to this recipe in 1979, when their original 40-year agreement to put it on their products expired. This was probably both to please time-pressed moderns and because of changes in baking ingredients. Most flour today comes pre-sifted and Wakefield's instructions to create a baking soda paste with water likely helped to activate it in a way that is no longer necessary with modern sodas. Food science expert Shirley O. Corriher says using a contemporary high-protein bread flour (closer to the all-purpose flour made in the 1930s) or a quarter cup more all-purpose flour than called for would lend your cookies their original heft. (Although in a 1975 interview, Ruth herself said she often used a quarter cup less flour to create "a more delicate" cookie.) In later editions of her cookbook, Wakefield gave instructions for shaping and baking the cookies the way they were in her Toll House restaurant (included here after the recipe). Wakefield's daughter, Mary Jane, today remembers with some amusement a whole series of promotional photos of her and her mom making the cookies that couldn't be used because "I had forgotten to squish the dough down" as per these instructions.

Ruth and daughter Mary Jane with non-squished cookies

- ★ Cream 1 cup butter, add ¾ cup brown sugar, ¾ cup granulated sugar, and 2 eggs, beaten whole.
- ★ Dissolve 1 teaspoon baking soda in 1 teaspoon hot water and mix alternately with 2¼ cups flour sifted with 1 teaspoon salt. Lastly add 1 cup chopped nuts and 1 pound Nestlé's yellow label chocolate, semi-sweet, which has been cut in pieces the size of a pea.
- ★ Flavor with 1 teaspoon vanilla and drop half-teaspoons on a greased cookie sheet. Bake 10 to 12 minutes in a 375-degree oven.

Makes 100 cookies

Note: To make the cookies according to later editions of the *Tried and True* cookbook, after forming the dough, refrigerate it overnight. Roll a teaspoonful of the dough at a time between the palms of your hands and space them 2 inches apart on the cookie sheets. Press the dough balls with your fingertips to form them into flat rounds. Bake for 10 to 12 minutes, or until brown and crispy. Makes 50 cookies.

Nestlé's yellow-label chocolate bar

By this time, chocolate had been used in baking for at least 30 years, including in cookies in Wakefield's own cookbook, but it was melted first. Most versions of the ran-out-of-nuts Toll House® invention story also say that Wakefield expected the nut-sized nuggets of chocolate to melt in the batter. But this part of the story is belied by Wakefield's household arts college degree and what reporter Hanes heard from the cook's mouth. "It was one year after a trip to Europe that she remembered some chocolate experiments she . . . made in a college food-chemistry class. She ordered some chocolate bars from the grocery [and] after testing and experimenting, she and her pastry cook, Sue Brides, came up with a new cookie."

1936 edition of Ruth's cookbook

And yet the no-nuts story continues to be told, even by Wakefield's daughter, Mary Jane—although at least she knew her mother well enough to know she would not have run out of nuts by accident. (In her version, there was a shortage of available nuts due to Depression-era shortages.)

Chalk up this myth's persistence to a lack of good information but also to modern Americans' love for the dumb-luck story. That Ruth Wakefield invented the chocolate chip cookie by dint of training, talent, hard work, and mind-expanding world travel made possible because she was already well on the way to earning her first half-million may not be as appealing a story to people who dream of lucking into the latest Lotto jackpot, Post-It Note invention, or YouTube viral craze. But it is the true one.

The cookie Wakefield and Brides invented also might not be all that appealing to modern chewy-gooey chocolate chip cookie fans. More in the mold of its austere English ancestor biscuits, Chocolate Crunch Cookies, in Wakefield's own 1948 words, "should be brown through, and crispy," hence the "crunch" in its name. Like its tea nut refrigerator cookie inspiration, the Crunch Cookie

And if You Liked the No-Nut Story, You'll Love the One About the Colonial Drop Do Cookie

If there is one constant in all the chocolate chip cookie invention stories, it is that Ruth Wakefield first added pieces of chocolate candy into dough made from a colonial butter drop do cookie recipe. This "fact" has shown up in Nestlé® promotional pieces for almost 50 years and also is engraved on the bronze plaque that was erected on the site of the Toll House restaurant under the old Toll House restaurant sign.

The Toll House logo screamed *colonial*

Which is curious, considering that the drop do lacks the chocolate chip cookie's distinguishing brown sugar and contains such other deal-breaker ingredients as rosewater and mace. Curious, that is, unless you've seen the 1960 Nestlé brochure "Tale of the Toll House® Cookie," in which a Nestlé copywriter links the colonial history of the Toll House restaurant building with one of two cookie recipes included in Amelia Simmons' *American Cookery* (1795), the first cookbook published in America.

A well-worn Toll House restaurant cookie sheet

Therefore the drop do is "probably the earliest ancestor of the Toll House cookie," the brochure asserts. In the Toll House cookie, "the spirit of colonial times shines through. Like the drop do, it still stands for hospitality, for kindness, for the good things in life."

Some later Nestlé publicist apparently missed the fanciful spirit of the brochure as well as the paragraph noting the many differences in the two recipes, and started spreading the idea that Ruth Wakefield literally added chocolate to the drop do recipe, as her Nestlé promotional heirs have ever since.

At least one Whitman-area historian also refuted the copywriters' premise that the Toll House restaurant building dated back to colonial times. Although the story that the Toll House had been a colonial-era toll house was pushed by the Wakefields and Nestlé alike (on menus, in Ruth's cookbooks, and via the 1709 date on the building's chimney), Martha Campbell wrote that the Cape Cod house actually was built by one Lebbeus Smith as a residence in 1817. While it was located on a toll road, no whaling captains or stagecoach drivers ever ate or stayed there. In fact, Campbell says the building only served food unsuccessfully for a few years before the Wakefields bought it.

While marine artist Frank Vining Smith did grow up there, the building's main claim on history remains as the birthplace of the chocolate chip cookie.

dough was chilled overnight. Several former waitresses remember a metal ring mold that was used to ensure the dough balls were all the same size (in case you don't already get what a perfectionist Ruth Wakefield was).

One of them is Sue Brides's daughter, Marguerite Gaquin. Brides died in 1966 and Gaquin's recollection of what she was told about the cookie's invention is foggy, but not contradictory. "She had a recipe for a cookie and decided to do something different with it," says Gaquin, who does remember vividly how red and sore her mother's hands got from cutting chocolate to make the cookies before chocolate chips were invented.

Sue Brides and other Toll House staff making the cookies

Gaquin also says she has the restaurant's recipe for Toll House® Chocolate Crunch Cookies and that it is different from the one Ruth Wakefield first published in the 1938 edition of her *Tried and True* cookbook, though she allows that the differences could have been born of World War II–era shortages. Gaquin will only definitely confirm that the restaurant recipe she got from her mother was made with Crisco instead of butter. She also deems the official version "too sweet" and gives a pained look at the mention of the published original's two eggs. Tasted side by side, Gaquin's Toll House cookies are lighter in both color and weight, crunchier, and not as sweet as ones baked from Wakefield's published recipe.

Even in its subordinate role as ice cream accompaniment, the cookie was noticed and appreciated by Toll House diners, and before long, the restaurant was handing out hand-typed copies of the recipe to its biggest fans. The first food professional to get one was General Mills home economist Marjorie Husted (aka Betty Crocker). At a Chicago restaurant meeting, Husted told Wakefield she wanted to start a new series of radio programs about famous American restaurants with a show on the Toll House. "I can remember we hooked up a little radio in the kitchen and stood around listening to Betty Crocker tell about the Toll House and about the recipe for cookies," Wakefield recalled during a speech to employees of Nestlé® predecessor company Lamont, Corliss in New York in 1941. But *Boston Herald-Traveler* food editor Marjorie Mills had a greater impact on the cookie's "spread." After Mills published the recipe and featured it on her radio broadcast, "We were just flooded with people writing," Wakefield said. Beginning in September 1938, the recipe was also making regular appearances in the recipe swap column of rival newspaper the *Boston Globe*—called variously Chocolate Crunch cookies, Toll House® cookies, and, as early as February 1939, chocolate chip cookies (perhaps because the cookies required cooks to chip the chocolate bars with a knife or ice pick).

Marguerite Gaquin, with a "real" Toll House cookie

Meanwhile, in New York, Lamont, Corliss executives saw sales of their previously sleepy Nestlé semisweet chocolate candy bar rise an astounding 500 percent in southern New England. The executive they dispatched to investigate ended up on Ruth Wakefield's doorstep.

The *Christian Science Monitor*'s Hanes said he was only one of a number of chocolate company representatives who showed up in hopes of getting Wakefield's endorsement. But since she had started out using the Nestlé product and was happy with it, on March 20, 1939, Wakefield gave Nestlé the right to use her cookie recipe and the Toll House name. "I signed off for a dollar—of course, you never see the dollar," Wakefield told magazine reporter Arthur Lubow in 1976, "wryly," is the way he heard it. "I was always brought up in college to think that a professional person doesn't enter the commercial world." Wakefield also consulted on recipes for Nestlé for years, probably for real money. Some say she got money plus free chocolate for life. Whatever the case, Nestlé got a good deal. The Toll House cookie was and still is one of few cases of a popular back-of-the-box recipe created by a customer rather than a company test kitchen. All Nestlé had to do was stroke the already existing excitement.

The company's first attempts to do that were text-only and hard to distinguish from the unpaid attention the cookies were getting elsewhere on newspapers' women's pages. They were also models of cross-marketing: In addition to the recipe and the admonition to "insist on Nestlé's® Semi-Sweet Chocolate in the yellow Wrap, there is no substitute," most also referenced the recipe source as "the famous Toll House Inn at Whitman, Massachusetts" and "Mrs. Ruth Wakefield's Cook Book *Toll House Tried and True Recipes*, on sale at all bookstores."

The suburban Cleveland Nestlé test kitchen named for Ruth Wakefield

The earliest display newspaper ads were in a Sunday comics format and targeted middle- to upper-class women who had lost their servants to factories or the belt-tightening Depression and were facing their stoves alone for the first time. In "Grocer Jones Tells All," a woman goes to the store to buy a ready-made version of the Toll House® cookies she has heard so much about, only to have Grocer Jones send her home with some Nestlé chocolate and assurances that "dozens of my customers use that recipe and they say it never fails." Although her family is initially skeptical ("Don't tell me Mother made it herself," her teenage daughter wisecracks on hearing of the evening's "dessert surprise"), the cookies win them over, with Junior asking for more in his lunchbox and cynical Sis giving Mom a congratulatory kiss.

In another cartoon drama titled "John Stayed Downtown Again for Dinner," Jane's mother counsels Toll House cookies as the answer to Jane's marital woes. "I'm glad your mother came by, Jane. These cookies she made are wonderful," enthuses husband John, safely ensconced at the dinner table. "Jane made them herself. I didn't show her a thing," his mother-in-law responds, with a conspiratorial wink to Jane. The comic's concluding panel shows Jane holding a glowing plate of Toll House cookies, John looking on with pride.

In these ads and the less wordy ones that appeared in national women's magazines at the same time, the Toll House® cookie is easy to make, universally popular, and, most important, the key to elevating "your reputation as a housewife."

At first Nestlé® was just advertising this new use for their old semisweet chocolate candy bar, though by late 1939 that bar's dozen eating "sections" had been subdivided into 160 scored pieces "just the right size for these cookies," as one recipe pamphlet explained. Toll House's teardrop-shaped "morsel" chips debuted in the cookie's home state of Massachusetts in December 1940 but not in the aforementioned national women's magazines until a full 13 months later. One possible reason for the delay: Due to sugar shortages in the build-up to World War II, "For the first morsels, substitute sugar was used. . . . It turned hard and people cracked their teeth on them," Nestlé executive Bill Bell later recalled.

Rival chocolate bar makers jumped in with their own ads or back-of-the-box chocolate chip cookie recipes almost immediately, as did makers of the Toll House recipe's other ingredients McCormick (vanilla), Spry (shortening), Nucola (oleomargarine) and Gold Medal (flour). By May 1941 there were also several competitive chocolate chip products and, wrote Jane Holt in the *New York Times*, "What with all of American manhood, from 6 to 60, clamoring for cookies with small bits of their favorite flavor—chocolate—flecking them throughout, this simple device is a boon to the hurried homemaker." Chocolate chips or morsels (as Nestlé called them) were the rare case of a food product invented for a specific recipe.

"How can you possibly bake cookies and cakes with unmelted bits of chocolate in them. It seems like magic!" reads one ad from chocolate maker Baker's, echoing the delight consumers in Nestlé ads expressed at finding whole pieces of chocolate candy in their cookies. In these days of Heath Bar ice cream and Oreo-stuffed cupcakes, the idea of enhancing one sweet with another

Why It's Not Baker's Toll House Cookies

Baker's chocolate was made right up the road from the Toll House in Dorchester, Massachusetts, and was the brand Ruth Wakefield planned to use the day she invented the chocolate chip cookie, she told magazine journalist Arthur Lubow in October 1976. "I had intended to use Baker's dipping chocolate . . . but our wholesaler didn't have any." So she took Nestlé's.

Thus are $350 million businesses made and lost.

A 1941 *Better Homes and Gardens* ad featuring Nestlé's® scored chocolate bar

might seem obvious but at the time, it was revelatory, to give Ruth Wakefield her due. Chocolate makers hoping for more than just a short-lived recipe fad heralded the Toll House® cookie as the dawn of a new age of "chocolate chip cookery."

In their free recipe booklet, "Chocolate Chip Cookery Comes to Town" the age-old Baker's chocolate girl herself was pictured chopping off pieces of Baker's Semi-Sweet Chocolate Bar with a knife to make the cookies as well as polka-dotted cake, candy and pudding. Not since "baked Alaska," had there been anything "so new and startling in the dessert line as these chocolate chip recipes," Baker's boasted. A similar Nestlé recipe pamphlet called semisweet chocolate cookery "the most talked-about baking discovery since lemon meringue pie."

Then along came World War II, which diverted chocolate to the troops and threatened to end the chocolate chip craze almost as soon as it had begun. In fact, production of Hershey's first chocolate chip for the retail market, Dainties, was discontinued shortly after its 1941 debut to make way for wartime products, and didn't return until 1948. Nestlé® ads encouraged patience with product shortages and repositioned Toll House® cookie making as an act of patriotism. "Now that Nestlé's Semi-Sweet Chocolate is harder to get . . . put it to the best possible use. Make up a batch of these golden-brown, crunchy Toll House cookies and send them to that soldier boy of yours," read one ad headlined "His One Weakness." One war-era Nestlé recipe brochure came complete with packing instructions and mailing label. Another, designed for those short on sugar rationing points, featured a recipe for Toll House cookies made with honey and maple syrup.

Judging from the number of references to Toll House cookies that pop up in newspaper stories at the time—it was the most popular cookie at the USO

This 1940 ad heralded the recipe's inclusion on Gold Medal Flour bags.

clubhouse in Hartford and with WAACS training in Des Moines, and what the girls at Hunter College in New York City spent a lot of their dateless nights baking—Nestlé® was once again only going along with what was already going on.

Wartime is also when Ruth Wakefield first began selling cookies out of her restaurant's "What Not" gift shop. "We have miniature Toll Houses, cookie filled (to be used later for flowers)," is the first menu reference (in 1941). A 1944 menu asks, "Wouldn't you like to send a box of Toll House cookies to your boys in the service?"

Thousands of Toll House® cookies were shipped from the restaurant around the world or served in Red Cross canteens during the war. George Boucher's son and former Toll House bus boy Dennis Boucher says this is when the standard recipe lost its nuts, because they would have gone bad on their

1942 Nestlé recipe booklet

The Non-Melting Morsel Miracle Explained

Almost all of the early ads for Toll House cookies expressed amazement that the chocolate stayed whole while cooking. Seventy-five years' experience has taken away the "wow" factor but still, if chocolate's melting point is about 90 degrees and most recipes call for baking chocolate chip cookies at 375 degrees, why doesn't the chocolate melt?

It does, actually, as you have plainly seen if you've ever pulled a hot-from-the-oven cookie apart (or seen one of Nestlé's many ads showing one being pulled). It's just that there's enough other stuff in the chocolate to keep it together until the cookie cools down and the chocolate becomes solid again, says Nestlé director of technical applications Jane Hardman. And if the chocolate has been tempered properly before you buy it, it will be none the worse for having gone through this solid-to-liquid-back-to-solid transformation.

1983 Nestlé ad spotlighting the melted chocolate

Should You Find Yourself in Massachusetts: Points of Interest on the Toll House®/Ruth Wakefield Trail

Wendy's, 362 Bedford St., Whitman, 781-447-2878. This is probably the only Wendy's restaurant in America that doubles as a museum. It was a concession Wendy's made to the town for allowing them to put their fast-foodery on the site of the storied Toll House restaurant, which burned to the ground in a dramatic fire near the end of New Year's Eve service on December 31, 1984. (So dramatic and storied, in fact, that footage from the fire still regularly airs on the Whitman public access television station.) Photographs of Ruth and some of the restaurant's most famous celebrity guests as well as newspaper accounts of its fireworks end line the walls; the sign with the trademark colonial bell ringer that used to grace the restaurant's front lawn now sits in the parking lot next to a historic plaque erected by Nestlé®. Warning: The chocolate chip cookies that Toll House pilgrims will be craving are not sold at this or any other Wendy's.

Wendy's "museum"

Ruth Wakefield's home, 487 Auburn St., Whitman. Although the Wakefields originally lived on the second floor of the Toll House, they soon bought this colonial-era house next door to make room for private dining rooms and offices in the restaurant. The adjacent Toll House Village condominiums take up land that once housed the restaurant's wishing well, outdoor gift shop and rambling additions, including the famous Tree Room.

Toll House Village condominiums

Former Toll House Motor Lodge, 519 Auburn St., Whitman. Though it was sometimes called an inn, the Toll House never had overnight accommodations, until the 1950s, when the Wakefields bought this nearby house with three rooms that was managed by longtime Toll House hostess Helen Morton. Former Toll House bus boy Michael Dion used to bring breakfast over to guests, including, once, to John F. Kennedy and a woman he says "was not Jackie." The lodge is now the private home of Theresa Healy and her daughter Brina, who pay tribute to the house's famed past with a back-porch shrine to the Toll House, including a framed copy of a 1930s Toll House menu, Nestlé Toll House cookie tins, a "Jack Kennedy Slept Here" plaque Theresa found when she bought the place, and a display case containing one of Ruth's old *Tried and True* cookbooks.

Lodge "shrine"

Ruth's second home, 59 Pill Hill Lane, Duxbury. The Wakefields moved from their house next door to the Toll

House to another one overlooking the bay at the end of a single-lane road shortly after adopting their first child in the early 1940s. (By that point, the Wakefields had already been robbed at gunpoint in their house behind the restaurant.) Although the spot was always prime waterfront, multiple additions and renovations by the subsequent owner have obscured the house's colonial core and made it much grander than when the Wakefields lived there.

Ruth's grave

Mayflower Cemetery, 225 Lincoln St. (195A Cypress Lane), Duxbury, 781-934-5261. Ruth shares this simple '50s-era gravestone with her mother-in-law, Katharine Harding Wakefield.

Gershom Bradford House, 931 Tremont St., Duxbury, 781-934-6106, www.duxburyhistory.org. A sundial on the lawn of this 19th-century ship captain's home not far from Mayflower Cemetery pays tribute to Ruth for her efforts in helping to acquire, refurbish and restore this and several other historic houses for the Duxbury Rural and Historical Society. "People trusted her and loved her, sometimes were a little afraid of her, for she gave so completely of herself that they could not always keep pace," fellow Society member Jack Post wrote after her 1977 death.

Sundial homage

Toll House Bakery, 25 Oak St., Abington, 781-982-2781, www.tollhousebakery.com. This small cookie dough–making spot, housed in the back of a transmission shop and mainly focused on cookie dough for fundraising, is all that's left of the Toll House restaurant's cookie-making activities, which had expanded greatly after the Saccone family took over the restaurant in 1973. But the 1984 fire, supermarket slotting fees and an expensive Nestlé® trademark lawsuit all took their toll, so to speak. Peaceful Meadows Dairy Store (60 Bedford St., Whitman, 781-447-3889) is one place in town you can buy this heritage cookie dough.

Henry Whittemore Library, Framingham State University, 100 State St., Framingham, 508-620-1220. Ruth graduated from the Household Arts department of what was then Framingham State Normal School in 1924, and donated her personal collection of about 120 cookbooks to her alma mater in 1969. They can be viewed by appointment. She unfortunately did not mark up her books, although the collection provides a clue to her culinary times and inspirations.

Sandwich Glass Museum, 129 Main St., Sandwich, 508-888-0251, www.sandwichglassmuseum.org. Ruth Wakefield once owned one of the country's best collections of colorful Sandwich glass. They were among the many tasteful antiques that adorned the Toll House. After selling the restaurant, she became volunteer curator of this museum, which still owns and displays some of her pieces.

Sandwich Glass Museum

long trip to the soldiers overseas. In 1975, Wakefield recalled hearing about a war-era royal Christmas party where a New England soldier presented Queen Mary with a box of Toll House® cookies. Like Spam and Coca-Cola, chocolate chip cookies' fame was boosted by wartime solder consumption. Before the war they were a largely East Coast–based fad; after, Toll House cookies rivaled apple pie as the most popular dessert recipe in the country.

Given that, it's surprising how relatively few references were made to the cookie by Ruth Wakefield or at the Toll House during the Wakefields' reign. The cookies are absent from a photo spread of the restaurant's famed desserts in the cookbook's 1940 revision. They get a single sentence in the Toll House's 21-page 1949 promotional booklet and only passing mentions in the ads and cover copy for her cookbooks in the mid to late 1940s (as in her publisher's 1945 boast that "the melting deliciousness of the famed Toll House Chocolate Crunch Cookies has been recaptured a thousand times over" in her book's many "wonderful recipes").

Toll House pastry staff, including Sue Brides (second from right), with their pride and joy

Wakefield talked cookies even less after she and Ken sold the restaurant in 1967, according to her daughter and Mary Alice Kirby, a Whitman resident who helped Wakefield with one of many community events Wakefield was involved with before and especially after her retirement. Kirby thinks Wakefield's silence on the chocolate chip cookie subject was partly because Wakefield had "moved on," and partly because "she had all these fabulous desserts, that you couldn't get anywhere else and could be quite involved to make. The cookies were more of a common thing that everyone made at home and that they just gave away."

Whatever the reason, it made it hard for Wally Amos to find Wakefield when he was looking for a chocolate chip cookie origins story to put on the bags of chocolate chip cookies he started selling in the late 1970s.

Cookie Title Fight

You might think that the unofficial cookie of America would be a shoo-in for official state cookie of the state where it was invented. That is, unless you know that the Fig Newton was also invented in Massachusetts, and was a favorite of the sitting governor when some school kids started pushing for the chocolate chip in 1997.

"When was the last time your mother baked you a warm batch of Fig Newtons?" one of those kids asked Governor William Weld, during the discussion in the State House.

"Fig Newtons are a form of self-punishment," argued another chocolate chip cookie lover in a Newton vs. Toll House® poll conducted by the *Boston Globe* at the time.

The Somerset, Massachusetts, third-graders took up the Toll House cause in conjunction with a class project where they created a business to sell chocolate chip cookies, and performed an original rap song at a legislative hearing advising representatives to "give the chip no lip."

Speaking for the other side was Stan Kurzman, a businessman in the Fig Newton's namesake Newton. "I don't like the Toll House cookie because it reminds me of the tolls I have to pay on the highways," Kurzman said.

Commenting on a phone poll that showed the chocolate chip way ahead, an aide to Newton state senator Lois Pines said, "That's because our people couldn't talk because they had their mouths full . . . chewing on Fig Newtons."

Ultimately the legislators and the governor bowed to the majority and in a July 9 ceremony attended by the inventor's daughter, Mary Jane Wakefield, and the school kids and fueled by Toll House cookies and milk, Weld signed a bill making the Toll House the official state cookie of Massachusetts. Being a skilled politician, Weld later that day threw a crumb to his losing side by introducing legislation proposing to make the Fig Newton the state's official *fruit* cookie.

Chocolate-chip-loving kids stare down William "Fig Newton" Weld

The Magical Toll House

By Richmond Talbot

Employees loved the Toll House. Despite—or maybe because of—the high standards, whole families worked there for generations. Adult diners were wowed by their wonderful service and great food. But kids were also entranced by the place, as Plymouth, Massachusetts–based writer Richmond Talbot explains in this charming reminiscence, first published in the Old Colony Memorial *newspaper in 1987.*

We only [went to the Toll House] on special occasions, but it was often enough for me to remember the grandfather clock by the front door. From there, you turned left into an anteroom decorated with antiques and were shown down some steps into the main dining room. What a place to impress a child! It had a huge tree growing right up through the roof. Sometimes our table was right by the ivy-covered trunk so you could see that it was absolutely real.

The Toll House understood children and offered each one a present. The knowledge of this raised the excitement of my arrival until it was almost too much to bear. On the way in from the parking lot there was a wishing well, and I was given a penny to toss in, but my wish didn't concern the present. I knew what would be offered, and always chose the same thing.

Sketch that adorned the Toll House menu

My early childhood was spent during World War II when rubber was a strategic commodity. It was restricted for civilian use and certainly not available for something as frivolous as a toy balloon. You couldn't buy one in any store, but the Toll House must have had a prewar supply stashed away because they always had them, and a balloon was always what I chose.

It was not a conservative choice. A child's relationship with a balloon always ends badly. My happiness was almost as fleeting as a taste upon the tongue, but I have the memory of those balloons to this day. The meals were also pleasures that could be saved only in memory, but they have stayed with me longer than my sturdiest toys.

On one of my first visits, I was served an appetizer of fresh fruit cup topped by a ball of sherbet. This was so astounding as to be beyond belief. I wasn't sure that eating ice cream before the rest of your dinner was even moral. Sometime later, I told my mother I wanted to go back to the place where they gave you your dessert first, and it took her some close questioning to figure out what I meant.

Of course, no kid would be willing to give up the dessert at the end of the meal on the flimsy excuse that he'd already had it, and at the Toll House, I didn't have to. There was something called a Mary Jane sundae, which was peppermint stick ice cream rolled in coconut and covered with hot fudge sauce. There was a special lemon pie with a meringue so tall, a wedge looked like a sailboat. There were also Toll House® cookies, but . . . my mother made Toll House cookies. When I ate out, I [was more interested in] things I couldn't get at home . . .

I'm putting this in a child's order of importance, so I'll get to the entrée in a minute, but first I want to mention the warm caramel-pecan rolls. They arrived right after you did and kept you amused until the waitress took your order and brought it to the table.

Toll House waitresses didn't say, "Hi, My name is Cheryl, and I'll be your server this evening." Instead of memorizing a spiel, they remembered everything that was ordered without writing it down and delivered each dish to the correct person without asking who got what. Large parties with people changing their minds didn't faze them a bit.

The dining room "had a huge tree growing . . . through the roof."

On my earliest visits, I always got creamed chicken. They served it in a white milk glass hen which added to my awe. . . . Later I graduated to Cape scallops, which were small and sweet and really came from the Cape.

The Toll House flourished before gourmet food came into fashion, and they didn't attempt the exotic. Their customers expected the kind of food they were used to, so the Toll House was content in serving it as close as possible to perfection.

I guess having a restaurant built around it wasn't good for the tree, because it died. The trunk still stood in the dining room, but branches no longer overspread the roof. Sometime later, the restaurant passed out of the Wakefield family, who had made it what it was.

It went through several owners but in other hands it was just a restaurant, nothing more. I didn't feel bad when the historic building finally burned. Like the tree, it had become a lifeless remnant of its former grandeur. It's better to remember the Toll House the way it used to be.

2

Chip Heyday

If the servantless masses of the ’30s and ’40s didn’t know how to cook, at least they were embarrassed about it. In the ’50s, this was no longer the case.

One of many cookie stores that sweetened American street corners in the 1980s.

Food companies anxious to find a new audience for the powders and pastes they had created for foxhole consumption found a willing audience in families who were now too busy raising the boomers to bake. Whether women did or didn't actually have more time than before the war, fussing over raw ingredients was no longer fashionable. Hence, the debut of Nestlé®'s Toll House® Cookie Mix (in 1955) and Pillsbury Refrigerated Chocolate Chip Cookie dough (in 1959). They were followed only four years later by the launch of the first major national brand of packaged chocolate chip cookies, Nabisco's Chips Ahoy, which Wally Amos knew about, but would not eat. In fact, up until age 33, Amos had never eaten any store-bought chocolate chip cookie.

from Betty Crocker
12 MINUTE
CHOCOLATE CHIP COOKIES
nothing to do but slice and bake
Betty Crocker
CHOCOLATE CHIP
Cookies
Refrigerated and ready to bake. You'll like Ginger Molasses and Raisin Oatmeal, too.
LOOK FOR THE RED SPOON
IN YOUR GROCER'S DAIRY CASE

Betty Crocker's 1961 dough debut

Growing up eating his Aunt Della's homemade chocolate chip cookies had spoiled him for any other kind, Amos explains in his *Famous Amos Story*. And it was not just because of his aunt's skills as a cook. Della was the loving aunt who took Wally into her Harlem home after his parents got divorced when he was 12, and the cookies were part of her expression of love.

"Somehow I must have thought I would never be without them, because I never got the recipe," Amos wrote. Della's nephew grew up to be the first black talent agent at William Morris, booking such high-profile acts as the Supremes, Dionne Warwick, and Bobby Goldsboro. But when he started his own talent agency across the country in Los Angeles, "I was at a loss because Aunt Della's cookies were no longer available. So I simply went without." Until one day when a client came into the office with some homemade chocolate chip cookies that tasted exactly like his Aunt Della's. Demanding the recipe, he was told that it was on the back of the Nestlé's chocolate morsel bag. That very night, he went to the store, bought the bag with the recipe and all the other ingredients, and baked his first batch.

The cookies soon became his edible

"calling card," something to sweeten his client pitches. Although everyone seemed to love them, and at least one business associate suggested he should sell the cookies for a living, he didn't seriously consider it until trumpeter Hugh Masakela let him go, another client used the money she owed him to lease a Mercedes-Benz, and a promising actor he represented fell and broke his leg just 20 minutes before he was set to star in his breakthrough role. Amos decided he had had enough of representing unpredictable humans.

Early Famous Amos bag

With financial backing from musical-superstar friends Helen Reddy and Marvin Gaye, among others, Amos leased a store on Sunset Boulevard in Hollywood next to the Exotica School of Massage ("Sindy's Nude, Nude, Nude Girls, Girls, Girls") and across the street from the American Institute of Hypnosis and the Seventh Veil Restaurant ("Home of Camel Juice"), that itself had been the former location of several failed restaurants. With the predictive optimism of a promoter, he dubbed his new cookie company Famous Amos. He staged the March 9, 1975 opening like a movie premiere, with cookies, champagne, music, and 2,500 guests, including lots of people who just pulled their cars over to see what all the excitement was about. He later staged his cookie's debut at a department store in Tucson, Arizona, like a visit from an important statesman, arriving in town in a helicopter dubbed "Cookie One," stepping out on the tarmac with one cookie nestled on a satin pillow, which his son held while sitting in a huge fan-shaped straw chair in the back of a pickup truck for the "motorcade" ride to the shopping center. Once there, Amos gave employees of a nearby ice cream parlor kazoos so they could serve as his musical honor guard.

In essence Amos became an agent for the chocolate chip cookie.

As with any human client, Amos felt "The Cookie" should have a bio. But when he set out to research its history to put on the cookie bags in those pre-Internet, pre–*The Great American Chocolate*

The original Famous Amos store

Parsley, Sage, Rosemary, and Chocolate Chip Cookies

If Wally Amos hadn't become famous for chocolate chip cookies, he might still be in the pop culture history books as the William Morris agent who signed an up-and-coming folk duo named Simon and Garfunkel.

So what did he see in them? "I was just floored—by the lyrics, the way their voices blended, by their look"—which was "like Napoleon and a tall guy whose hair looked like he had just stuck his finger in a light socket," Amos said, remembering back to the 1964 recording session where he first heard them perform. "They were unique and if you're different, you're at least going to get people's attention. And if there's substance there as well . . . and Paul was a gifted songwriter who was able to transfer the concerns of the people to song."

Chip Cookie Book days, all he could find were some references to it having been invented in Massachusetts in 1929 or 1939. Fusing this information with Amos's prior association with blues singer Lowell Fulsom, Amos associate Chuck Casell dreamed up a fanciful story of how the chocolate chip cookie was born "in a tiny farmhouse kitchen in Lowell, Massachusetts" on what "has come to be known as Brown Thursday."

Pretend premiere parties and welcoming ceremonies are one thing; but Lowell was a real place. Far from a farm town, Lowell was actually the birthplace of the American Industrial Revolution. While getting a history lesson from the Lowell city fathers, Amos finessed an invitation to the former mill town, thereby getting his cookies and Lowell a whole bunch of positive publicity. (The Lowell folks also told Amos about Ruth Wakefield, though she died before they could connect.)

Amos's powers of persuasion were also on display in a 1983 *Newsweek* profile that described him working a sidewalk outside one of his stores. "Fa-mous Amos!" he sang to the tune of the Hallelujah Chorus, a leather chocolate chip cookie bag

Famous Amos's Original Chocolate Chip Cookies

Unlike his fellow 1980s cookie moguls, Wally Amos has never made any secret of the recipe that made him famous: It was Ruth Wakefield's, only made with margarine and pecans and originally, a little bit of coconut. He has published both his recipe and advice on how to bake his cookies, the most unorthodox being his recommendation to talk to your cookies while they are baking. "Tell them you love them, and that it's important for them to get as brown on the bottom as they are on the top. Let them know they are about to bring a lot of joy and pleasure to people." And while you're at it, give a quick shout-out to the baking sheet. Eat these cookies like Amos does, with yogurt, fruit juice, a fruit smoothie, or champagne.

1 cup (2 sticks) margarine (Amos used Blue Bonnet)
2 large eggs
1 teaspoon vanilla extract
¾ cup packed light brown sugar
¾ cup granulated sugar
2¼ cups all-purpose flour
1 teaspoon vanilla extract
2¼ cups all-purpose flour
2–4 tablespoons grated coconut (depending on how much you like that taste)
1 cup pecan pieces
3 cups (18 ounces) semisweet chocolate chips (Amos used either Nestlé® or Ghirardelli)

Preheat the oven to 375 degrees. Unwrap the margarine and grease two baking sheets with the margarine paper. In a large bowl, cream the margarine, eggs, vanilla, brown sugar, granulated sugar, soda, and salt. Add the flour—gently!—and then the pecans. Add the chocolate chips (which Amos calls "the most important ingredient") only until the chips are well integrated. Drop by teaspoonfuls onto a baking sheet about an inch apart. (Famous Amos cookies should be bite-sized.) Bake for 8 to 12 minutes, watching the cookies closely and turning the baking sheets several times. Leave on the baking sheets for 2 minutes, then transfer to wire racks to complete cooling.

Yield: 80 to 100 cookies

Wally Amos in Macy's Thanksgiving parade

dangling from his shoulder. "Here, have a Famous Amos cookie. I am the Famous Amos. Whoop! Cookie time here, cookie time! I am Famous Amos and there's my store right there. Oh, please take my cookies! How can I sell 'em if I can't give 'em away . . . Hey, we got two left. One for you . . ."

Famous Amos was (and is) charming. He was also one of America's first famous black businessmen (a fact obliquely referenced by his "Have a very brown day" salutation). Both probably explain how he ended up on the cover of *Time*, in the Smithsonian (via his trademark panama hat and embroidered gauze shirt), and as recipient of a Small Business Entrepreneurial Award from President Ronald Reagan—despite never actually having made a profit on his cookie business.

Amos himself has admitted that he was a much better pitchman than businessman or even baker. Cookies from his first store were terrible, Amos explains in his book *The Cookie Never Crumbles*, until someone pointed out that he had gotten the sides of his new kitchen scale reversed and so was using way too much flour.

Moving to Hawaii also probably wasn't the best business decision, he later

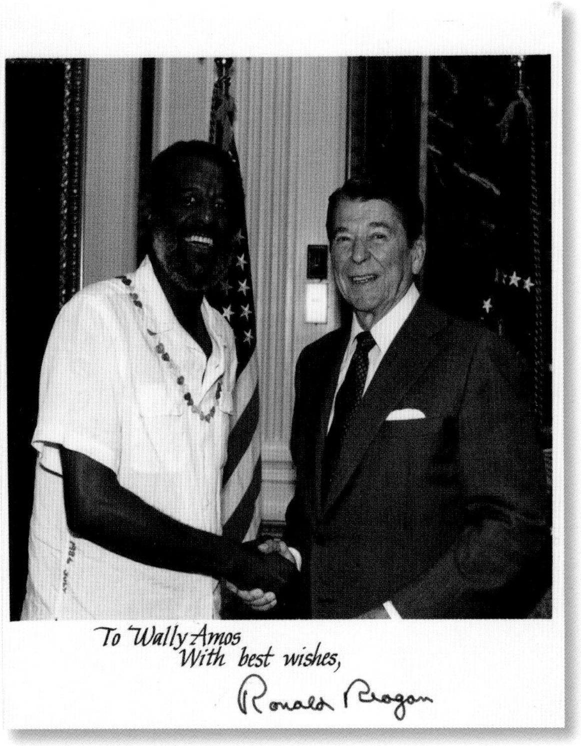

Wally and Ronnie, BFF

admitted, especially doing it at the time when his business was about to be threatened by another famous 1970s cookie entrepreneur.

In 1977, Debbi Fields was the 20-year-old trophy wife of Randy Fields, an economist 10 years her senior whom she had met in a Denver airport on her way back from a ski trip. In her autobiography, *One Smart Cookie*, Fields describes a dinner party at the home of arbitrager Sandy Lewis that changed her life of leisure.

Although her husband's colleagues were usually content with her role as eye candy, this day Lewis seemed intent on engaging her in a serious conversation, culminating with a question about what she intended to do with her life. A rattled Debbi replied that she was mostly "trying to get orientated."

Lewis grabbed a dictionary from his big bookshelf and tossed it at her with disdain. "The word is oriented. There is no such word as 'orientated,'" he spat. Debbi was devastated. She cried for hours afterwards. But when the tears stopped, she was a stronger and different Debbi, determined to do something with her life and the chocolate chip cookie recipe she had been perfecting since age 13. (See "Miss Sivyer's Cookies," page 47)

Her parents were not supportive, citing her total lack of business experience. The only bank loan she could get was at an outrageous 21 percent interest. Even her economist husband bet she wouldn't have $50 in her cash drawer by the end of the first day. And by noon of the first day she opened Mrs. Fields' Chocolate Chippery in an international food court in Palo Alto, California, not far from Stanford University, she had not sold a single cookie.

Desperate, she took to the street, giving away samples, discovering in the process that on average, every fifth free

Debbi and husband Randy working at the very first Mrs. Fields store

cookie resulted in a sale. By the end of the day she had her $50; on day two, she had $75. She was on her way. And the sampling she did on that very first day become part of the rulebook for her cookie-store chain. (When Debbi was in charge, 4 to 12 percent of all Mrs. Fields cookies were giveaways.)

The cookies Mrs. Fields served were almost the exact opposite of the ones Famous Amos was selling 300 miles south. Where his were cute and small, hers were big and thick. Where his were crispy (as was then customer preference), hers were soft. Where Famous Amos's best-seller featured pecans, Fields's customers so preferred macadamias that it

Miss Sivyer's Cookies

The very first consumers of Mrs. Fields Cookies were umpires at Oakland Athletics games in the early 1970s. The then–Debbi Sivyer, 13, was working as a foul line ball girl for the A's. Flamboyant team owner Charlie Finley liked the homemade chocolate chip cookies Debbi shared with the A's office staff so much that he had her serve them to the umpires between innings. This and her ability to look cute in the skimpy uniform presumably made up for her other shortcomings: "I don't believe I ever caught a single baseball," Fields has admitted.

Bogus Mrs. Fields Cookie Recipe

Anyone over 40 has undoubtedly heard the story: A woman calls Mrs. Fields cookie company headquarters in Park City, Utah, and asks if she can buy the recipe for their chocolate chip cookies. After some hemming and hawing, the company representative agrees to send it to her for two-fifty. The woman gives her credit card number and a few days later gets a copy of a chocolate chip recipe in the mail—and when she receives her next credit card bill, a charge from Mrs. Fields for $250. Rebuffed by a Mrs. Fields representative when she calls to complain, the woman makes a thousand photocopies of the recipe and sends it out as a chain letter. "This is a true story! Please send this to every single person you know."

This is NOT a true story but it was a huge public relations problem for Mrs. Fields in the mid-'80s—so much so that she eventually posted signs in all her stores denying the rumor and saying that the company's recipes were a "delicious trade secret" that were not for sale. It is actually just one iteration of one of America's most persistent urban legends. Urban myth scholar Jan Harold Brunvand says a very similar story was told about a red velvet cake recipe sold for $100 at the Waldorf Astoria hotel in the 1940s. In the mid-'90s, a variation on this cake story, involving cookie eaters at the Neiman Marcus store café in Dallas, clogged American's email boxes. Brunvand says the story persists because it taps into Americans' distrust of big business, their interest in secrets, and also because the recipe itself isn't half-bad. On that last point, Debbi Fields disagrees. She tried the recipe at the height of the rumors and declared the cookies dry and heavy (probably because of the oatmeal, which her chocolate chip cookies don't contain), although I know some people who like them.

1 cup unsalted butter, softened
1 cup granulated sugar
1 cup packed brown sugar
2 large eggs
1 teaspoon vanilla extract
2½ cups rolled oats
2 cups all-purpose flour
1 teaspoon baking powder
1 teaspoon baking soda
½ teaspoon salt
2 cups (12 ounces) semisweet chocolate chips
1 (4-ounce) Hershey milk chocolate bar, grated fine
1½ cups chopped nuts

Heat the oven to 375 degrees. Cream the butter with the granulated sugar and brown sugar. Beat in the eggs and vanilla. Blend the oats in a blender or food processor until powdery. Stir the oats, flour, baking powder, soda, and salt into the butter mixture. Add the chocolate chips, grated milk chocolate bar, and nuts. Form the dough into balls almost twice the size of golf balls and place on ungreased baking sheets about 2 inches apart. Bake for 10 to 11 minutes or until small cracks form on the cookie tops. (If you wait until the bottoms are totally brown, the cookies will be overbaked.)

Yield: 24 large cookies

Unofficial but Closer to the Real Mrs. Fields Cookie Recipe

The Mrs. Fields recipe hoax may have been a business-breaker for Mrs. Fields but it was a life-changer for Todd Wilbur. Seeing the popularity of what he realized was a bogus recipe woke him up to America's hunger for food trade secrets and led him to launch his career as a creator of copycat corporate food recipes published in his best-selling *Top Secret* cookbooks and website (www.topsecretrecipes.com). In fact, the Mrs. Fields chocolate chip cookie recipe was the very first recipe Wilbur ever tried to re-create.

Debbi Fields meets her public

Mrs. Fields didn't sell or give away its company recipes in the 1980s, and it's not about to today. But Mrs. Fields the company founder did publish one of her personal favorite chocolate chip cookie recipes in her best-selling cookie book. The following Mrs. Fields chocolate chip taste- and lookalike is informed by that recipe, Wilbur's sleuthing and an interview where Mrs. Fields told me, "I baked my cookies at a lower temperature for a longer time" and stuffed them with so much chocolate "they almost wouldn't hold together."

2¾ cups all-purpose flour
1½ teaspoons salt
1 teaspoon baking soda
1 teaspoon baking powder
1¼ cups (2½ sticks) cold unsalted butter, cubed
¾ cup packed light brown sugar
¾ cup granulated sugar
2 large eggs
1 tablespoon Madagascar vanilla extract
3 cups semisweet chocolate chips (65 percent cacao content or higher)
1½ cups chopped macadamia nuts (Mrs. Fields's signature nut—see page 50)

Combine the flour with the salt, baking soda, and baking powder. Using an electric mixer, beat the butter, brown sugar, and granulated sugar until completely blended. Beat in the eggs and vanilla. Add the flour mixture to the wet ingredients and mix just until combined. Mix in the chocolate chips and nuts. Refrigerate for at least 2 hours.

Preheat the oven to 300 degrees. Line two baking sheets with parchment paper or foil. Place ¼-cup portions of dough on the baking sheets, 3 inches apart. Press down on the dough with your fingers and shape it so that you have disks about ¾ inch thick and 2½ inches in diameter. Bake for 25 minutes or just until the cookies start to brown around the edges. (They will appear underbaked but take them out anyway.) Immediately transfer the cookies to wire racks; let cool for 5 to 10 minutes.

Yield: 20 cookies

wasn't long before she was buying almost 10 percent of the world's supply. Fields developed her fondness for macadamias while vacationing in Hawaii, and started making her cookies big to deflect her mother's (and later, her husband's) questions about the number of cookies she was eating. Like Amos's, Fields's business grew out of her genuine love for the cookies, which she preferred a bit underdone.

This key attribute was captured in one of her chain's many aphorisms: "Mr. Thumb lives in every store." Mr. Thumb? "When a team member lifts a cookie before selling it, the person must depress the bottom of the cookie with the thumb—we call it Mr. Thumb—to make sure it is absolutely soft," Fields explained to *Los Angeles Times* reporter Bettijane Levine in 1993.

Mrs Fields with employees

Mrs. Fields and the Mystery of Ala Moana

At its peak, Mrs. Fields had almost 700 stores. But they almost stopped at number three. It was at the Ala Moana Shopping Center in Honolulu in 1980 and after the grand opening ceremony, the store went dead. The recipes and ingredients were checked; the store amped up its sampling program, but still, sales were miserable. "We wondered out loud if maybe we hadn't hit the wall in terms of expansion," Debbi Fields wrote in her autobiography, *One Smart Cookie*. Then a Fields company executive happened to mention the problem to a friend who had grown up in Hawaii. "Did you have a kahuna bless it?" the friend asked, referring to the Hawaiian priests who routinely appear at new businesses to sprinkle water and chant prayers.

The company immediately found a kahuna to do the blessing. The day after the ceremony, crowds of cookie lovers appeared. Ala Moana went on to become one of the chain's most profitable stores.

A Hawaiian store blessing

Stories are legion of store visits where Fields would throw out hundreds of dollars' worth of cookies that she deemed less than perfect. Cookies more than two hours old—cookie "orphans" in Mrs. Fieldspeak—were given to charity rather than sold. Fields's standards for customer care were similarly high. Shy or not-sufficiently-enthusiastic potential employees were weeded out as part of hiring process requiring them to eat a cookie, give away some cookies, and sing "Happy Birthday," out loud in the store. (Hires would eventually be caroling from the Mrs. Fields songbook of cookie musical parodies like "Chip-a-Dee-Do-Dah," after all.)

The company's phenomenal early success was, by most accounts (including an admiring 1988 Harvard Business School case study), also due to a software program husband Randy invented that gave managers of the chain's 600 outlets instant access to what Debbi had learned running her own cookie store. For instance, the program could help a manager set a baking schedule based on the weather and past year's sales for that day and offer suggestions for unloading more cookies if cash register input was not living up to history.

Debbi Fields's personal appeal was also a factor, as it was for Wally Amos. "She succeeds because she is a good person. I've seen her stop her car and help a little old lady carry her groceries," Randy Fields once said (before their divorce). Unlike most other commercial baking icons (read Betty Crocker, Mrs. Smith, Aunt Jemima), Mrs. Fields was young, blonde, and attractive enough that men would not immediately switch to the game if she was on TV. Women thought, "If she can own a cookie company and look like that, well, what's the harm in having just one of her cookies?"

The third member of the 1970s cookie entrepreneur triumvirate was a nonpracticing New York lawyer who had worked at the famed Troisgros restaurant in France and had moderate success selling gourmet cooking sauce bases to home

A David's Cookies supermarket display

chefs. Although David Liederman's Saucier products had no competition—and maybe because of it—people found the product hard to understand and, as Liederman wrote in his 1989 business book, *Running Through Walls*, "I finally realized that I could not educate the public to what this product was all about without a lot of money that I didn't have. So I went to a product that I felt Americans understood—chocolate chip cookies . . . and twisted it a little bit."

Liederman had checked out Famous Amos's Hollywood operation—his twist was to use butter instead of margarine, and hand-chopped chunks of Lindt bittersweet chocolate, rather than Nestlé® morsels. His cookies were flat and chewy, rather than round and crispy like Famous Amos's or warm and gooey like Mrs. Fields's. David's Cookies was only one of dozens of cookie stores in New York City when it opened at Second Avenue and 53rd Street in the summer of 1979, a framed, notarized statement from David's mom, saying that "cookie" had been David's first word, on the wall. The store struggled for a month with almost no business. Then Florence Fabricant of the *New York Times* declared David's the best cookies in the city and suddenly Liederman had to struggle to keep up with the demand. For a month anyone who came to the shop after lunch was greeted by a sign reading, "Out of cookie dough, come back in three hours."

David Liederman with his cookie dough

Liederman went on to become friends with Fabricant and many other journalists who kept his business in the public eye. And it's not hard to figure out why. Liederman is a great interview. Consider his response when a reporter questioned him about his chain's policy of charging for a cup of tap water: "Maybe it's because a large number of robberies in the stores are

David's Makes the Very Best–Roast Chicken?

When David Liederman went looking for a space for his very first David's Cookie store, he fell in love with a too-big place on Second Avenue near 54th Street in New York City that the landlord wouldn't subdivide. So he took the whole thing and put a cookie store on one side and a restaurant on the other. Originally the restaurant was the nouvelle cuisine Manhattan Market. But by 1985, it was Chez Louis, Liederman's tribute to the L'Ami Louis bistro in Paris. Many New York City old heads are today as nostalgic for Chez Louis's roast chicken as they are for David's original cookies. See David's Chez Louis chicken recipe at www.foodnetwork.com. Here is my stab at his recipe for chocolate chip cookies.

Chocolate Chunk Cookies Something Like the Old David's

2 cups all-purpose flour

1 teaspoon salt

1 cup (2 sticks) unsalted butter, melted

1 large egg plus 1 egg yolk

1¼ cups packed brown sugar

2 teaspoons vanilla extract

14 ounces 70 percent cocoa chocolate, coarsely chopped (Liederman used Lindt Excellence)

Mix the flour and salt together in a small bowl. In a large bowl, thoroughly cream the butter, brown sugar, egg and yolk, and vanilla. Stir the flour mixture into the butter mixture. Fold in the chocolate chunks. Refrigerate for 3 to 4 days (the time necessary, Liederman has written, "for the vanilla flavor to permeate the eggs and the chocolate").

About an hour before you're ready to begin baking, take the batter out of the refrigerator to bring it back to room temperature. Line two baking sheets with parchment paper or foil. Preheat the oven to 400 degrees. Form the dough into 1½-inch balls, place them 2 inches apart on the baking sheets, and squish the balls down to the size and thickness cookie you want. Bake until golden at the edges and still soft in the center, 10 to 15 minutes, depending on how you shaped your cookies. Let the cookies cool on the baking sheets for 5 minutes then transfer to wire racks to cool completely.

Yield: 36 cookies

Why There Are No Packaged Nestlé® Toll House® Cookies

Although you might think Nestlé Toll House brand packaged cookies could give Chips Ahoy and Pepperidge Farm a run for their butter and sugar, it's not going to happen, at least not on current Toll House brand marketing director Jim Coyne's watch. Here's why:

"Ask a billion people what a Nestlé Toll House is and they will come up with the same, very specific list: Warm. Chewy on the inside, crisp inside. Buttery brown sugar. Gooey chocolatiness.

"There's a vast difference between that and anything in a bag that sits around on a supermarket shelf for months," says Coyne.

Noticeable by its absence: Nestlé Toll House.

generated by people coming in and asking for a glass of water and then sticking a gun at the manager's head."

Liederman also spoke openly about inside crime. "Honesty does not seem to come naturally to many people. Employees think it's OK to take things home with them at night because the store is popular and no one will notice. Even when people do notice, employees take things. Sometimes it is cash. The only way to stop stealing is for the owner to actually be there."

Moreover, Liederman has counseled, nobody ever got rich overestimating the intelligence of their employees. "One of the reasons we do so well in the cookie business is that a chimpanzee could take cookies out of that bag and more often than not [prepare them properly]," he once said.

A chimpanzee, maybe, but not all people. In his book, Liederman tells of visiting a David's kiosk in a Florida department store and seeing "six different varieties of perfectly scooped David's cookie dough sitting on trays in the sales case. "Nobody told me you have to bake them," the employee responded, when Liederman pointed out the problem.

Compare that to how Debbi Fields talked about her employees in a July 1984 *Inc.* magazine story: "People come to work because they need to be productive. They need to feel like they are successful in whatever they do. . . . When you make the cookie and you sell the cookie and the person says, 'This is great. This is better than homemade' . . . that fuels the individual to do a great job because he doesn't want to let the customer down."

"Everybody likes to be made to feel special and important. . . . That's my real role. To make people feel important and to create an opportunity for them. That's really my role as the cookie president, the cookie person."

"That airhead," Liederman called Fields in that same story, before airing his suspicions that Mr. Fields was really running the company. But today Liederman says at least some of that bad-mouthing was for show. "I liked Debbi. We both made a fortune off of my hating Debbi Fields."

David's, Mrs. Fields, and Famous Amos were only among the largest and most enduring of an estimated 1,200 cookie stands generating an estimated collective half a million dollars in retail sales by the mid-1980s. Famous Amos's trendy treat for the Hollywood elite had by then spread so that virtually every street corner in the country had an Original Great American Cookie Company, Famous Chocolate Chip Cookie Company, Carol's Cookies, Tom's Mom's, Cheryl's, the Original Cookie Company, Cookie Bouquets, Ultimate Cookie, Blue Chip Cookies, the Cookie Factory, The Cookie Caper, Cookie Place, The Cookie Works, The Cookie Muncher, Unknown Jerome, Zaro's Cookie Corner, The Cookie Factory, The Cookie Store, Got Your Cookie, Kiss My Cookies, Otis Spunkmeyer Old Tyme Cookie, The Chipyard, Cookie Coach, or Captain Cookie. Cookie Coach had 31 reproductions of 1901 bakery carts equipped with artificial chocolate chip cookie–scent machines selling the real thing from Wall Street to East 86th in Manhattan; Captain Cookie was delivering 15-pound, 2½-foot cookies in the same area for $150 each. (Read more about some of the surviving companies in chapters 3 and 4.)

And the 1980s cookie wars were not limited to retail cookie stores. Makers of packaged supermarket cookies also tried to cash in on the craze with cookies that mimicked the texture of fresh-baked. Although Procter & Gamble (P&G) food scientists began working on this idea in 1976, Frito-Lay beat them to market by a year with their Grandma's Cookies in 1982. Procter & Gamble then scrambled to introduce their Duncan Hines chocolate chip cookie made with two doughs—one that baked up crispy surrounding another that stayed chewy. (And yes, this Duncan Hines brand was started by the restaurant reviewer who so loved Ruth Wakefield's Toll House.) Nabisco and Keebler followed with Almost Home and Soft Batch, respectively, quickly thereafter.

One 1980s soft-cookie-war survivor

Suspiciously quickly, to P&G's lawyers, who, in a 1984 lawsuit, charged all three of the other companies with stealing their secret crispy-chewy technology. P&G claimed Nabisco had sent a spy to a contract manufacturer to study up on their processes and accused Keebler of taking aerial photographs of their half-built Jackson, Tennessee, cookie plant. Frito-Lay admitted to obtaining both a factory photo and a dough sample but, like the kid who stumbles onto his Christmas presents early, promised that they did not peek.

Cookie lovers in the soft cookie test market of Kansas City who were showered with free samples and money-off coupons, and lawyers who worked the case all grew fat in more than one way. The 200 witnesses in the legal battle ranged from a German kitchen equipment manufacturer to a Pillsbury Bake-Off winner. Julia Child and the women behind *Food that Really Schmecks*, a 1968 cookbook containing an Old Order Mennonite recipe for a two-dough cookie that had the potential to invalidate P&G's patent, were also pursued as witnesses, albeit unsuccessfully (the latter, because Old Order Mennonites are forbidden from participating in court proceedings).

The case was eventually settled for $125 million, which was the most ever paid in a patent infringement case up to that date, although it was only a fraction of the money these four companies ended up burning up on soft cookies. Never having made cookies before, Frito-Lay and Procter & Gamble took on the expense of buying or building factories. Established cookie companies Nabisco and Keebler amped up their advertising to unprecedented levels to combat the newcomers.

But when the advertising stopped, so did sales. The cookies may have had the soft texture of home-baked and retail store cookies but as one industry consultant observed at the time, "the packages tasted better than the product."

Love Chips Ahoy? Let Us Count the Chip Number Claims

The easiest way to make people like your chocolate chip cookies? Overload them with chocolate chips. No wonder, then, why Chips Ahoy's oceanful of chocolate chips has been at the heart of promotions for this most popular of packaged chocolate chip cookies for almost its entire history.

The claims date back to Chips Ahoy's 1960s "Cookie Man" advertising campaign, which featured a mild-mannered accountant type whose chip counting would be interrupted by some cookie-eating monster, requiring his transformation into Cookie Man. The concluding tagline? "Chips Ahoy: the 16-chip cookie."

The brand reacted to the sales-threatening retail cookie stores of the early 1980s by doubling chip content from 16 to 32 (later scaled back to 24) and changing the slogan to "Betcha Bite a Chip."

By the mid-'90s the ad focus broadened to talking about the whole "1,000 chips delicious" bag, a claim that some third graders in little Wadesboro, North Carolina, decided to test during arithmetic class in 1996. Finding 680 chips at the max (and in some bags much less) they fired off 130 letters of protest to Chips Ahoy baker Nabisco. "You told us a lie and that was not nice," said one. "Would you PLEASE stop cheating people?" asked another.

Countdown Wadesboro participant Kimberly Bennett, 8

Confident that their factory chip-weighing equipment was in order, Nabisco executives volunteered to stage a public recount in Wadesboro using bags of Chips Ahoy purchased at a local supermarket.

And as it turns out, these kids and their teachers only counted the chocolate chips they could see on the surface of the cookies. Tutored in the technique (favored by food professionals and toddlers alike) of soaking the cookies in water so the chips could separate out, the kids counted 1,181 chips, a finding announced during a press conference covered by *The Today Show*, *ABC World News Tonight*, the *NBC Nightly News*, *CBS This Morning*, *Newsday*, and the *Wall Street Journal*—or more media outlets than covered the O. J. chase, the opening of Al Capone's vaults, and Prince Harry's visit to Las Vegas combined.

Nabisco saw Chips Ahoy sales jump almost 20 percent as a result and not surprisingly soon staged a "1,000 Chip" counting contest promotion that attracted an entry from some U.S. Air Force cadets—which should be a comfort to anyone who thinks the greatest threat to U.S. national security to be a dearth of chocolate chips.

The Cookie's Cartoon Pitch-Creatures

Did the chocolate chip cookie become popular because of its association with the Pillsbury Doughboy and Ernie Keebler or did the Doughboy and Ernie become famous because of their association with a popular cookie?

It's hard to say but there's no doubt that kids' huge influence on supermarket cookie purchases has made cartoony characters popular with the ad folks charged with promoting cookies.

The Doughboy was created in 1965 to introduce Pillsbury's new Crescent Roll dough; Leo Burnett agency copywriter Rudy Perz envisioned him as the personification of the Crescent Roll dough popping out of the can, hence the Doughboy's nickname, Poppin' Fresh. But within the year, he was also hawking Pillsbury's chocolate chip cookie dough. Perz brought his dough man to life by giving him a scarf, a chef's hat, two big blue eyes, and Carey Grant's charm. He'd blush when a little girl gave him a kiss and when people gave him an affectionate poke in the stomach, he'd cut loose with a funny little giggle. In cookie ads, the Doughboy pops up mainly to do a lot of wordless nodding and pointing.

A rulebook running hundreds of pages reins him in more than the strictest parent would. Talking, eating, showing his backside, or tricking people are all out, and help explain why Pillsbury passed on a fun "Got Milk?" ad that was to show the Doughboy mischievously washing down his cookies with the last of one family's supply of milk (although he was later allowed to appear in one with a Russian family, with the mom who forgot to replenish the family's supply of "moloko" playing the heavy).

Cookie advertising magic struck the Leo Burnett agency again only a few years later, in the guise of the Keebler elves. In 1966 the United Biscuit consortium of regional bakeries decided to unify under a single brand name and ad campaign to help them compete with much bigger competitor Nabisco. Rather than downplaying Nabisco's dominance, Burnett decided to play up the David and Goliath situation with a campaign that implicitly pitted the huge, impersonal Nabisco baking factory against the little elves who lovingly baked cookies in their hollow tree home. The first ads showed a succession of human skeptics investigating the claim, a catchy jingle explaining the setup and the tagline, "Uncommonly good, wherever they come from."

But they didn't include Ernie Keebler. The first chief elf was the pompous, businesslike J. J. Keebler. He was briefly replaced by a golf-playing, wisecracking slacker named Ollie. But in Ernie, Burnett found a blend of innocence and simple goodness to match the Chips Deluxe chocolate chip cookies the elves made.

The good times at Keebler have "uncommonly" coincided with a high corporate elfin consciousness, including Keebler's mid-'90s turnaround under president David Vermylen. In 1999 anyone reaching his voicemail heard, "This is David Vermylen, a friend of Ernie Keebler, and I'm away from the Hollow Tree right now."

It's also perhaps worth noting that the beloved animation studio behind *Rocky and Bullwinkle* and Quaker's Cap'n Crunch commercials also created the detective character and ads for Mr. Chips, Quaker's long-gone cookie division's long-gone answer to Chips Ahoy. You'll have to ask your friendly neighborhood Jay Ward scholar to explain the reason for Mr. Chips's Secret Mission to Eyesore—although I can tell you it had nothing to do with an English boarding school.

The cookie store craze did inspire one successful line of supermarket cookies: Pepperidge Farm's American Collection of Mrs. Fields–sized decadent, more expensive variations on the all-natural crispy chocolate chip cookies they already made. Conceived in 1985 on the advice of consumer oracle Faith Popcorn (who divined cocooning *and* the soft-cookie-sales dive), these "lumpy, bumpy" cookies became one of Pepperidge Farm's most successful new product launches ever. (See "Gum Tree–Famous Cookies," page 61.)

In 1984, Nestlé® offered a whole family of Sweeties morsel-shaped plush dolls as purchase premiums.

The boutique Brent & Sam's brand of Famous Amos–style small gourmet chocolate chip cookies also debuted at about this time. The original Toll House restaurant also got into the act, expanding supermarket distribution of Ruth's small mail-order cookie business enough to catch the attention of Nestlé®, who sued for trademark infringement.

This sign marks the spot where Famous Amos got his start

The question is, Why did chocolate chip cookies become so popular in the 1980s and why are so few of the retail cookie shops that opened then still open today? One industry analyst theorized that high-priced cookies were part of the upscaling of all things childish for adult baby boomers, Peter Pan–like figures then just realizing their full earnings potential. (Designer blue jeans, running shoes, and video games also became popular at this time.)

A booming economy also helped people swallow the store cookies' then-high $5-a-pound price tag. That became harder after the 1987 stock market crash and resulting crumbling of the economy. The stores were also hurt by the decline of the malls where so many of the chain cookie stores were located, the rise in rents in urban locations, and cookie makers' inability to make the leap from a single bakery to a multi-outlet business, especially in the face of all the competition.

Although the chocolate chip cookie itself remained popular, the habit of stopping to buy it at a cookie store eventually gave way to stopping to buy subsequent fad foods like gourmet coffee, cinnamon rolls, and frozen yogurt. Or, with the rising health consciousness of the late 1980s and early 1990s, not stopping to buy these kinds of high-fat, high-calorie treats at all.

The first entrepreneur into the cookie market was also the first out. Between

The New Apple of America's Eye Is Apple

In a sign of the times, the Liddicoats building where Debbi Fields opened her very first Mrs. Fields cookie store at 340 University Avenue in Palo Alto was demolished in late 2011 to make way for a new prototype Apple store.

Gum Tree–Famous Cookies

All-natural food products are all the rage today but no preservatives and no artificial ingredients have been characteristic of Pepperidge Farm products since the company's 1937 start, a result of Margaret Rudkin's desire to find baked goods that would not exacerbate her son Mark's asthma.

Mark's doctor had advised Rudkin to restrict her son's diet to foods without additives. Since all commercial breads then had them, Rudkin decided to make her own stone-ground whole-wheat loaf. That doctor was so impressed that he recommended her bread to some of his other patients and thus a bakery was born. She named her company Pepperidge Farm after some sour gum trees that grew on the 125-acre Connecticut estate where she started her business (first in her garage, and then in some larger, converted horse stables).

Rudkin only added cookies—also all-natural—to her offerings in 1955, but they soon grew to account for half of her business. At first the cookies were elegant European ones, produced with the help of the Delacre company in Belgium. But when an "Old-Fashioned" American line was added in 1959, chocolate chip with pecans was among the first varieties. The pecans disappeared at some point, and the chocolate chip variety was phased out with the introduction of the larger, chocolate chip focused American Collection in the mid-1980s. As with the original Delacre "Distinctive" cookie line, American Collection varieties are named for locales familiar to people who can afford Pepperidge Farm cookies (e.g. Nantucket, Sausalito, Tahoe, Montauk)—having an American Collection cookie named after your town reportedly being better for property values than having Oprah as a neighbor.

Margaret Rudkin with chef and cookies

Pepperidge Farm's early '80s chocolate chips

Freezer King

The mid-'80s craze for the chocolate chip cookie also showed up in the freezer case in the form of the Chipwich, 3½ ounces of premium vanilla ice cream sandwiched between two soft chocolate chip cookies, its edge studded with yet more chocolate chips.

This world's first premium ice cream novelty was invented by a CBS video engineer with some Coney Island pitchman experience, an ownership stake in an Englewood, New Jersey, ice cream shop and the desire to recreate his lifelong love of dunking chocolate chip cookies in milk in frozen form.

Richard LaMotta (cousin of *Raging Bull*–profiled boxer Jake) labored at the ice cream shop and his father's Brooklyn basement for a year in the late 1970s before figuring out how to put the ice cream and cookies together in a way that didn't leave the cookie soggy. Englewood mom Ann Dermansky won a $10,000 college scholarship for her daughter and a year's supply of Chipwiches in the contest that gave the novelty its name.

LaMotta had originally planned on introducing the Chipwich in supermarkets, but while eating a hot dog he bought from a street vendor after a discouraging meeting about doing that, he got the idea to sell his ice cream sandwiches in upscale street carts. He raised the necessary $500,000 by approaching "everyone I knew with one hand grasping a cooler of Chipwiches and the other held out for money. It got to the point where . . . people started ducking into stairways when they saw me," LaMotta recalled later.

On May 1, 1981, 60 people in Indiana Jones–wear took to the Manhattan streets with red-and-white umbrella carts to sell the 7-inch, 4½-ounce frozen behemoths for a then-outrageous $1. But like the Haagen-Dazs ice cream that had debuted in supermarkets the decade before, adults ate LaMotta's creation up. In only two hours, the entire first day's supply of 25,000 Chipwiches was eaten. By the end of that summer Chipwiches were selling at the rate of 200,000 a day, and LaMotta's creation rivaled the Rubik's Cube and the Sony Walkman as a Reagan-era pop culture phenomenon.

By summer 1982, though, there were dozens of Chipwich copycats chipping away at LaMotta's business, including Chilly Chip, whose distributor told the *New York Times*, "One guy comes up with a good idea, and everybody rips him off. It's the American way." Several lawsuits and bankruptcy filings later, LaMotta sold the company to Eskimo Pie–maker CoolBrands, who, in turn, sold the brand to Nestlé®. They discontinued Chipwich in favor of their competitive Nestlé Toll House® Ice Cream Sandwich. Which is why you won't see and can't buy a Chipwich anymore.

LaMotta, who put on 30 pounds promoting his product, died (of—I hate to say it—a heart attack) in 2010 but should be remembered fondly by fans of chocolate chip cookies and any of the premium ice cream novelties (DoveBar, Magnum) that Chipwich paved the way for.

DIY Chipwich

The original ice cream cookie sandwich is now almost too obvious to need a recipe. Today the fun and excitement around this no-longer-really-novel ice cream novelty is in the creative pairing with the many new ice creams and different sauces. Chocolate chip cookies spread with Nutella sandwiched with maple walnut ice cream, or paired with dulce de leche ice cream and dipped in dark chocolate, anybody?

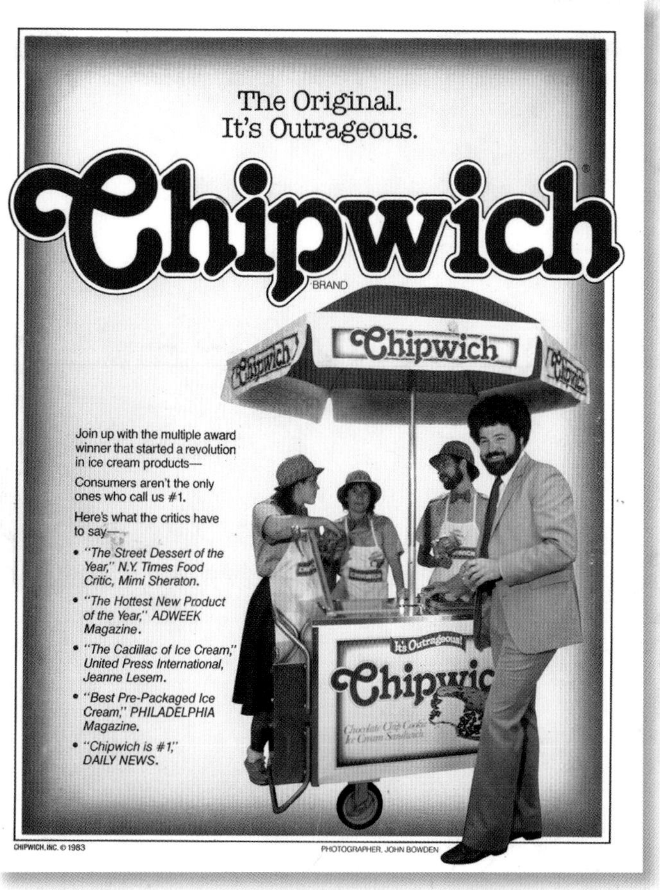

Ad featuring Richard LaMotta and one of his Chipwich carts

1 cup mini semisweet chocolate chips, candy, crushed cookies, or crushed nuts

16 large (3- to 4-inch), sturdy chocolate chip cookies, bakery-bought or bakery-style homemade (see recipes on pages 49, 95, and 111)

½ cup Nutella, caramel sauce, walnut sauce, peanut butter, raspberry jam, etc. (optional)

1 quart premium or super-premium vanilla (or other favorite flavor) ice cream, softened slightly

Put the chocolate chips in a medium bowl. Slather the flat side of one cookie with Nutella, if using. Place 3 to 4 tablespoons ice cream on the flat side of the other cookie, then top with the first one, flat side down. Press lightly until the ice cream just starts to ooze out the sides. Roll the ice cream edge of this cookie sandwich in the bowl of chocolate chips. Repeat with the remaining cookies. Eat immediately or wrap and freeze for later consumption. If freezing, let sit at room temperature at least 15 minutes before eating.

Yield: 8 sandwiches

A contemporary Mrs. Fields store

1985 and 1989, Famous Amos's company was sold four times, each time leaving Amos with a smaller piece of the business. In 1992, Wally Amos was so unhappy with the quality of the cookies then being sold under his name—mainly in vending machines—that he launched a new gourmet cookie company called Uncle Noname (to get around a non-compete clause he had signed).

By 1988 both David's and Mrs. Fields had diversified their offerings—he began selling ice cream and pizza in his shops and cookie dough in supermarkets; her stores were beginning to incorporate bagels and sandwiches from the La Petite Boulangerie chain Mrs. Fields had just acquired. This was also the first year the Mrs. Fields company lost money. By the mid-'90s neither Liederman nor Fields owned the companies that bore their names.

Today Mrs. Fields is probably as much known for its mail order, convenience, and even dollar-store products as it is for its freestanding retail stores. David's Cookies is a major player in food service, supplying cookies, cookie dough, and other desserts to restaurants and cafeterias all across the country, although Liederman says these desserts are not based on his original, all-natural recipes.

As for Famous Amos, his identity is as much a mystery to most of the people who buy the yellow bags and boxes bearing his name as Ruth Wakefield once was to Wally Amos.

The Common Taste

Successful politicians are at one with their electorate. That's one way to explain the large number of politically prominent Americans who love the country's most popular cookie.

That love starts at the top. Although perhaps more famous for his fondness for jelly beans, President Ronald Reagan also always had chocolate chip cookies on hand, at the White House and when he was traveling, according to his personal secretary. In his cookbook *Dessert University*, White House pastry chef Roland Mesnier said he baked chocolate chip cookies almost every day of a 24-year tenure that spanned the Carter, Bush 1 and 2, Reagan, and Clinton administrations. (See page 82 for more on modern-day First Ladies' cookie recipes.) Presidential hopefuls Ron Paul and John Kerry have also professed their love for this cookie. Republican rising star Bobby Jindal is so aligned with the treat that his chocolate chip cookie recipe is on the Louisiana governor 's official website.

Old Nestlé newsletter

Secretary of State John Kerry is actually among a half dozen politicos who have put their money where their mouths have been, literally. (Read about Kerry's adventures as a cookie mogul on page 98.) Former U.S. senator John Tunney was part of an investors group that got controlling interest of the Famous Amos cookie company in 1985.

And former U.S. senator Dale Bumpers owned 10 percent of his son Brent's Brent & Sam's cookie company before they sold to Snyder's-Lance. Brent & Sam's had its beginnings in the chocolate chip cookies that cook Liza Ashley made for Brent and childhood friend Sam DeWitt when Dale was the governor of Arkansas. Later, when they were all grown up and working as an assistant attorney general and a telephone company executive, respectively, Brent and Sam talked about building a business around that delicious recipe. When Ashley told them she was just using the one on the back of the Nestlé® bag, the friends challenged one another to come up with something better. The one they settled on was—and still is—a lot like Famous Amos's original. In fact, Brent has admitted that he and Sam once posed as tourists to take a tour of a Famous Amos cookie plant in Van Nuys, California (an episode sure to become campaign fodder should he ever decide to follow his dad into politics).

And then there is Michael J. Coles of Atlanta, who, in 1996, used some of the $60 million he made building his Great American Cookie Company to fund a failed campaign to take Georgia's Sixth District Congressional seat away from Newt Gingrich.

Coles started his cookie chain in 1977 with only $8,000 and, what's perhaps even more impressive, built it into a successful business despite suffering a near-fatal motorcycle accident that same year. Doctors warned he could be in a wheelchair for life. Instead, he parlayed leg-strengthening stationary bike exercising into several championship transcontinental bicycle treks, fueled, I assume, by lots of chocolate chip cookies.

The Cookie Titans Q&A

Wally Amos

Debbi Fields Rose

David Liederman

No one was more important to the chocolate chip cookie than its inventor. But Wally Amos, Mrs. Fields and David Liederman pushed this cookie's popularity into the 21st century. Where are they today? Not in charge of their old businesses but still very interested in the cookie of their mutual interest as you can see from the following Q&A created from separate recent telephone interviews.

Why is the chocolate chip cookie so popular?

Wally Amos: Chocolate chip has always been America's favorite cookie. Chips Ahoy helped to create that years ago.

Debbi Fields Rose: In part, it's because it's so common and well known. It's like vanilla, chocolate, and strawberry ice cream. Once people find something they love, they're not inclined to try something they've never had before.

David Liederman: [The chocolate chip cookie] is the Apple computer of sweets.

How does it feel to be associated with such a beloved American icon as the chocolate chip cookie?

WA: I am not associated with the cookie, I AM the cookie. My personality is part of that cookie; the cookie is an extension of my personality. It is infused by my warmth, spirit, and love. Being made with the highest-quality ingredients, it represents my beliefs.

DFR: I love it. Most people have a very positive association with cookies, nostalgic feelings about baking them with their grandmother or getting served them by their moms. . . . To have the chance to recreate that experience for others—what could be better?

DL: I could care less.

What do you think of the cookies now being sold under your name?

WA: I am not a fan. I really have nothing to do with that [Famous Amos] cookie [made by Keebler].

DFR: I do not believe the company now upholds the same standards we did. I haven't tried [the packaged Mrs. Fields cookies sold in convenience stores] but I know some people who have and say they're good. But I don't agree with it. They're not fresh, warm and hot. There might be a way to do a packaged cookie but it would have to be made with the utmost quality.

DL: I would never make that kind of garbage. They're using ingredients I can't even pronounce, the cheapest chocolate—that's why they're making a fortune.

Do you ever think about getting back into the cookie business?

WA: As a matter of fact, I'm putting a new company together as we speak. As part of the agreement I made when I sold my old company, I can't use the words Wally, Famous, or Amos, so my new company is going to be called WAMOS, with the tagline, "From the recipe that made me famous." I'm known for quality cookies and that's what these are going to be.

DFR: The [Mrs. Fields] company has a new CEO and . . . he wants to talk to me about coming back. That business is my heart. My name's on it and I never lost an ounce of care about it. If they're willing to do it my way . . .

DL: I am starting a new business to make the perfect cookie. It'll be called Liederman's Cookies. Studies show that 80 percent of home ovens aren't calibrated correctly, so I'll sell them an oven that will make the perfect cookie in eight minutes, along with the dough.

Everything I Learned About Life I Learned from My Cookie Business

Debbi Fields and Famous Amos have both enjoyed major second careers on the lecture circuit. People find their rags-to-riches stories inspiring. Being in the cookie business in particular seems to have brought out the Zen in them. Here's a taste of some of the wisdom groups and businesses pay as much as $25,000 to hear.

From Debbi Fields:

Good enough never is.

The biggest failure is not to try.

You've got to have fun or life is like one big dental appointment.

You can't pay people to care. You can instill in them your philosophy and values and pride. And you can pay them fairly. But doing a good job? That has to be their personal quest.

[Don't] be so afraid of disapproval—if people think you are doing the wrong thing it's not necessarily the end of the world. People aren't always right.

Big projects usually have all their history on board before they ever sail . . . It seems, at the beginning, like the future is a big mystery, but if you take careful note of everything that goes right and everything that seems wrong or difficult, you'll probably have a pretty good idea of how the story is going to unfold.

From Wally Amos (maker of cute little chocolate chip cookies):

Big is not better. Big is just bigger.

When I was involved with show business, I had designer suits with vests . . . The more I dressed like that, the more I wanted. One day I said to myself, "I don't want to be a big shot. I want to be happy." From that moment on, I started to be happy.

If you make a mistake, it's not the end of the world. Life goes on.

The key is for you to have the courage to be who you are in any situation, and not let circumstances or other people's behavior inhibit or diminish you.

The degree to which you succeed is directly related to the strength of your commitment. . . . Just about everyone I talked with about opening a store selling chocolate chip cookies had a reason why it would not work. If I had listened to any one of them, I never would have sold my first cookie.

3

Cookie for a New Millennium

By the late 1980s, it was increasingly hard to buy a chocolate chip cookie in its own dedicated retail shop shrine. But that doesn't mean chocolate chip cookies were hard to find. In fact, before the turn of the new century, warm and gooey chocolate chip cookies were available in virtually every place you could buy food in America, as well as some places that had never sold food before.

McCookies

Otis Spunkmeyer was among the major companies behind the change. Like Mrs. Fields, Spunkmeyer started in 1977 with a single California retail cookie store. Founder Ken Rawlings's 12-year-old daughter, Kimberly, came up with the oddball name, a fanciful amalgam of hometown football player Otis Sistrunk and popcorn maker Orville Redenbacher. By 1987, it had grown to a chain of 23 stores. But Rawlings saw the beginning of the end of the retail cookie store craze much earlier than his competitors, and, in fact, that year he sold his stores to Mrs. Fields to focus on supplying frozen cookie dough to restaurants, convenience stores, and cafeterias. And when those traditional markets were saturated, they marketed to any business where warm cookies might be seen as a comfort or incentive—traditionally banks, hotels and real estate offices, although car repair shops, jewelry stores, doctors who aren't that hung up about nutrition, even funeral home operators have also all signed on.

Ken and Linda Rawlings of Otis Spunkmeyer

When potential customers told Rawlings they didn't have the equipment or know-how to bake cookies, he threw in convection ovens and sales materials advertising his Otis Spunkmeyer brand. But the smell of baking cookies was the brand's most effective advertising. Under this business model, Spunkmeyer's sales grew 50 percent every year between 1987 and 1992.

Otis Spunkmeyer bag

Like Nestlé®, Pillsbury, and David's post-David Liederman, Otis also sold lots of its dough incognito,

The High-Flying Otis Spunkmeyer Company

Its kid-bestowed name is only one of the more fun—and some would say wacky—ways Otis Spunkmeyer achieved high-flying success. Another was Otis Spunkmeyer Air, two World War II fighter planes emblazened with the Otis Spunkmeyer name that regularly roamed the skies in the San Francisco Bay area between 1987 and 1999.

"My wife's a white-knuckle flyer," company president Ken Rawlings explained to a newspaper reporter in 1991, speaking of Linda, who was also his business partner. "But she felt so comfortable, at home, and safe" while taking a joy-ride on a DC-3 "that we decided to get one." And then another.

The older of the two was then the most historic plane in existence that still flew. The personal command post of five-star general "Hap" Arnold during World War II, its famous human cargo included Franklin D. Roosevelt, Winston Churchill, Dwight D. Eisenhower, and the queen of England.

Although originally mainly a side air-tour business (hour-long rides cost $100 and included era-appropriate music, wine, champagne, and, of course, cookies), the low-flying, slow-moving propeller-driven curiosities also generated Goodyear-blimp-like publicity, which company COO John Schiavo exploited in 1996 with an aeronautically themed Otis Spunkmeyer marketing campaign and new line of "Barnstormin' Bagels." Hap's C-41 also took part in a 50th-anniversary D-Day commemoration in Normandy, France, in 1994 (although between dodging low-altitude obstacles and refueling stops, it took the plane a week to get there).

But don't bother scanning the skies for Otis in San Francisco today. The planes were sold in 1999, not coincidentally the same year as a likely more practical investment firm gained majority interest of the company.

One of Otis Spunkmeyer's DC-3s

including to Subway beginning in the early 1990s. Three-for-a-dollar freshly baked cookies also took their rightful place beside such other American classics as hamburgers and apple pie at fast-food icon McDonald's at about the same time.

By the mid-'90s, there were also more chocolate chip cookie–buying options in the supermarket. Up until then the Doughboy had been a bachelor in the supermarket refrigerator case. But a steady decline in home baking, including baking chocolate chip cookies with Toll House® morsels, prompted Nestlé® to come out with its own refrigerated dough product featuring its chips. Ads touted Toll House's real semisweet chocolate, causing Pillsbury to switch from artificial to real chocolate bits in its best-selling chocolate chip cookie dough. Even more category-shaking were the new flat "Break and Bake" dough packages Nestlé debuted in 1999. Originally developed by a European Nestlé company for use with another kind of cookie, the pre-scored dough slab was much less messy than the rolls. Although it had never been rocket science, making cookies from refrigerated dough was now virtually idiot-proof: Just break off the dough squares at the scores and place them on a cookie sheet. Kelly Malley, a Nestlé executive on the Toll House brand at the time, said the equal-sized pieces of dough were particularly popular with "moms with multiple kids because it eliminated the fights over who was getting the bigger cookie." Adding to the fun was how the square blocks of dough baked up round—something that Nestlé showcased in their time-lapse TV ads.

Nestlé's® revolutionary Break and Bake dough package

The new packaging stole Pillsbury dough buyers, increased purchases by former Toll House tube dough customers, and also attracted people who had not bought refrigerated dough products in the messy old tube format, thereby eventually more than doubling Nestlé's share of the cookie dough market. Not surprisingly, the flat package is today the favored format for refrigerated cookie dough products industry-wide.

The Food Network also debuted in the

Sweet Land of Levain

It's only 11:30 a.m. but already a steady stream of people are making their way down the stairs into the tiny basement space that is Levain Bakery, many speaking excitedly in foreign accents or languages. Is 74th Street that close to the United Nations? Many pull out cameras or use cell phones to take pictures of the cookies on the counter or of their friends eating the cookies in front of the window outside.

That's because, according to the guidebooks many of these tourists are carrying, this tiny bakery is the home of the best chocolate chip cookie in New York City, if not the entire United States.

In fact, a Rio de Janeiro newspaper's recently published list of the top three things to do while visiting New York City were visiting the Metropolitan Museum of Art, touring Central Park, and eating a chocolate chip cookie at Levain Bakery.

Levain is also famous among chocolate chip cookie–loving Americans, although unlike the other most famous place (Tate's), Levain's owners did not set out to become the 21st century's Famous Amos.

Pamela Weekes and Connie McDonald met at a New York City pool when both were training for an Ironman competition. Looking for something to keep their energy and weight up that tasted better than power bars but were equally easy to carry on a bicycle, they began experimenting with chocolate chip cookie recipes. Weekes worked in the fashion industry and McDonald in banking but both were interested in doing something different. After McDonald took some culinary classes from Peter Kump, Weekes joined her in launching a wholesale bread-baking business out of a restaurant kitchen. In 1995, they moved operations to a retail basement space in a brownstone on the Upper West Side they dubbed Levain, after the French name for bread starter.

They did indeed start with only bread, including some poor-selling red grape and rosemary focaccia (customers mistook the sliced grapes for hot dogs) but later added

Levain Bakery owners Connie McDonald and Pamela Weekes

cookies that were a neighborhood favorite, especially the 3-inch-wide, 1-inch-tall, crunchy-on-the-outside, gooey-on-the-inside chocolate chip monster they had developed while marathon training.

Then in fall 1997, Amanda Hesser wandered in and wrote a piece for the *New York Times* calling theirs "the largest, most divine chocolate chip cookies in Manhattan."

"That was it for the cookies," Weekes recalled later. "For a month afterward, the shop would be chock-full, with people lined up on the stairs and down the sidewalk," many clutching that article. *Oprah*, a chocolate chip cookie *Throwdown with Bobby Flay* (they won) and the guidebook mentions followed. Levain is also currently the top-rated New York City restaurant on www.tripadvisor.com, despite, as Weekes points out, "not being a restaurant."

Foreigners come for the chance to experience something as quintessentially American as a Broadway musical and the Statue of Liberty; locals, for the cookie's huge size, pure ingredients, and, at a time when even high-end fooderies do-ahead, the way the dough is prepared daily and baked throughout the day. Any cookie not sold by closing is donated to what now have to be some of the city's most popular food banks.

Levain continues to supply its neighborhood customers with bread and other pastries, and the owners have not franchised the cookies or even published a cookbook. They have opened two Levain branches, including a summer-only shop in the Hamptons only about 10 miles from fellow chocolate chip cookie titan Tate's. Taking a cue from all the tourist picture-taking, they also launched LevainCam, cameras at both the 74th and Hampton shops that take photos of counter transactions that visitors can download off the Web. It's an instant ad that drives traffic to their website's mail-order store, which needs all the help it can get. Laments Weekes, "To get cookies this heavy shipped while they're still fresh is crazy expensive."

To the charge that the shop's cookies, at $4 each, are also pricey and bigger than necessary, McDonald says, "Any smaller and the cookie's texture would not be the same. And they're meant to be shared."

Adds Weekes, "Four dollars might seem expensive for a cookie. But it's not expensive for something to do in New York City."

'90s, and *The Dessert Show with Debbi Fields* was one of its very first shows. In 2000, mad food scientist Alton Brown devoted an entire still quite well-known episode of his popular *Good Eats* Food Network show to altering a basic chocolate chip cookie recipe to please his fussy TV sister Marsha. More recently, New York bakery Levain has "thrown down" Bobby Flay, been *Unwrapped*, and baked one of the best things Rocco DeSpirito ever ate, thereby benefiting from the channel's famed ability to make chefs, their businesses, and, in this case, their chocolate chip cookies, famous. (See "Sweet Land of Levain," page 74.)

But it took old media *New York Times* to turn the chocolate chip cookie into a new media star.

David Leite

In late 2007 freelance food writer David Leite was fishing around for a follow-up to a popular *New York Times* dining section story he had written about fried clam stands. He said then-editor Pete Wells's first reaction to his pitch for a chocolate chip cookie story was a wince. "What can you add to what's already out there?" is what he asked me," Leite recalled recently. Leite spent the next four months chatting up New York City bakers to come up with the four new ideas for improving on Ruth Wakefield's recipe that became the basis of his July 9, 2008 story, titled "Perfection? Hint: It's Warm and Has a Secret." It was the most-shared story on the *New York Times* website that day and that week (California wild fires, the G8 summit's greenhouse-gas agreement, and Maureen Dowd be damned). Nine months after the story ran, food bloggers were still making and commenting on the recipe. When *Cook's Illustrated* magazine weighed in with a fussy chocolate chip cookie recipe of their own in May 2009, the posting started all over again, comparing them.

In part, it was because of the chocolate chip cookie's inherent popularity; in part, reader outrage at the arrogance of the *Times* and *Cook's Illustrated* in claiming to have created a recipe better than Ruth

Getting Your Levain Fix In Between NYC Trips

This recipe incorporates elements of several online attempts to replicate the Levain cookie. The one at www.sugoodsweets.com has gotten more than 300 comments since it was first posted in 2006, including a popular alternative version by one "Lisa" and a few complaints about the cookie's blandness (note the lack of vanilla), with which I don't agree. To me, this cookie is all about multiple textures made possible by its large size. So don't try making this smaller. If you want small, make some Famous Amos (page 44).

1 cup (2 sticks) unsalted butter, cold
1 cup granulated sugar
¼ cup packed brown sugar
2 large eggs
2 tablespoons molasses (not blackstrap)
3¼ cups all-purpose flour
1 teaspoon salt
1 teaspoon baking soda
2 cups (12 ounces) Valrhona or other extra dark bittersweet chocolate, cut into chunks
1 cup walnuts, toasted and chopped (see page 166 for toasting instructions)

Levain Bakery case

Preheat the oven to 375 degrees. In the bowl of an electric mixer fitted with the paddle attachment, cream together the butter, granulated sugar, and brown sugar until well blended and fluffy. Add the eggs and beat until well incorporated, then add the molasses, flour, salt, and baking soda. Gently fold in the chocolate chunks and walnuts. Transfer the dough to a clean work surface, divide into 12 equal portions and form each portion into a loose ball. Place the balls on two sheet pans lined with parchment paper, six to a pan, and bake 13 to 18 minutes, rotating the sheets halfway through the cooking time, or until the outsides are tan.

Yield: 12 monster cookies

New York Times Recipe Takeaways

What did David Leite's 2008 *New York Times* story add to the store of chocolate chip cookie–making knowledge? Mainly the following four things:

1. Making your cookies big (at least 5 to 6 inches) results in an interesting range of textures, from crisp on the edges to ooey-gooey at the center.
2. Use thin disks of couverture chocolate—the high-fat coating chocolate candy makers use—instead of chips or chunks and the chocolate will melt into your cookies in layers. On the downside: The more desirable, higher-cacao varieties of this chocolate, sometimes called pistoles or feves, are pricey and can be hard to find.
3. Salt can heighten the flavor of sweets. To up its impact, use a generous amount of the coarse kind in the recipe and a sprinkling on top.
4. Letting your prepared cookie dough sit in the refrigerator for 24 to 36 hours before baking allows the ingredients to meld together to yield a richer, more complex flavor. (Don't go any longer than three days, though, or your cookies will just end up tasting stale.)

See page 166 in the recipe chapter for other tips on taking your chocolate chip cookies to the next level.

Visit the *New York Times'* website (www.nytimes.com) or Leite's own *Leite's Culinaria* (www.leitesculinaria.com) for Leite's complete legendary recipe.

Cookie chef's secret weapon

Wakefield's, or their own. The monster-cookie-sized reaction was also probably a reflection of the way people cook in the Internet age. If baking has long ago stopped being a daily habit in America, when people do take the time to bake, they want to use the absolute best ingredients and recipes. And now, thanks to the cooking shows and the Internet, that information and those products are ready at hand.

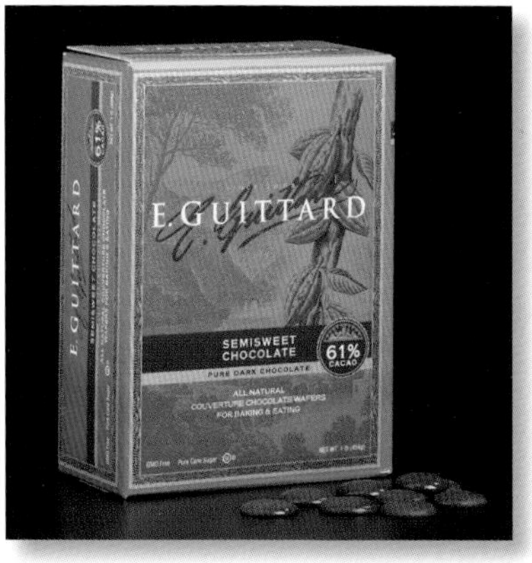

Guittard semisweet chocolate couverture wafers

Men, especially, seem to approach chocolate chip cookie making with the fetishism previously reserved for chili or barbecue. "I don't think anything can top chocolate chip cookies as the source of the greatest number of baking obsessions," confirms popular blogger and self-confessed chocolate chip cookie lover David Lebovitz in his 2010 cookbook, *Ready for Dessert.* Chief among chocolate chip cookie makers' obsessions is the quality of the chocolate chips or chunks. Ruth Wakefield would probably be amused to see how many modern American foodies have returned to laboriously cutting up chocolate bars by hand to get just the chocolate they want.

Leite actually recommended using disks of couverture chocolate in the *Times* recipe after the kind New York chocolatier Jacques Torres uses in his cookies. Next to that product's price tag and limited availability in the hinterlands, the biggest complaint about the *New York Times* recipe was with its idea that the dough needed to age in the refrigerator for 24 to 36 hours

Calvin and Hobbes on eating cookie dough

Movie Theater Concession Star

In 1992, recent business school grads Scott Samet and Douglas Chu launched their Taste of Nature company with the noble intention of putting healthy snacks into movie theater bulk candy containers. It took them less than three years to realize that action-flick-loving teens who make up the bulk of the American movie-going public didn't care a fig for dried fruit, trail mix, and pretzel sticks.

Familiar with Ben & Jerry's hit cookie dough ice cream (see nearby story), they figured chocolate-covered cookie dough candy had similar sales potential. So, in 1997, they launched Cookie Dough Bites in individual movie-theater-sized boxes (so they could sell them in theaters without bins as well as convenience and drug stores). A hit on its own, the product has also spawned a whole family of bakery treat facsimile candies, including Cookies 'N Cream Bites, Cinnamon Bun Bites, and Cupcake Bites.

The only question now is why their company is still called Taste of Nature and not Taste of Fat and Sugar.

Douglas Chu and Scott Samet with Cookie Dough Bites

before baking to achieve full flavor. Bloggers wrote that they couldn't (or didn't want to) plan their cookie-eating that far in advance, and those that could complained that they would end up eating the dough before it was baked.

Ah, yes, raw-cookie-dough eating. Ben & Jerry's had identified and exploited this underground subset of chocolate chip cookie consumption to great profit more than 15 years before with their megahit chocolate chip cookie dough ice cream. But that product is made with pasteurized eggs, thereby eliminating the possibility of salmonella poisoning from raw eggs—one reason your mother didn't like you eating out of the cookie dough bowl (the other being, obviously, fewer cookies for her!).

Cookie dough eating became a serious subject in 2009, when 77 people were sickened after eating Nestlé's® refrigerated cookie dough. Stories about the outbreak, which was eventually traced to *E. coli* in the flour (the only ingredient Nestlé was then not either pasteurizing or processing), noted that 66 percent of the victims were teenagers, mostly teenage girls, who had eaten the dough raw. One study has shown that more than half of college students of both sexes do the same thing. Today, there are more than 40 cookie dough fan groups on Facebook, with more than 12 million members.

The Flavor That Put Ben & Jerry's in the Dough

As if being America's most popular cookie wasn't accomplishment enough, the chocolate chip cookie is also the basis for one of the 20th-century's most popular ice cream flavors.

That would be, of course, chocolate chip cookie dough ice cream and within two months of joining Ben & Jerry's supermarket pint lineup in 1991, it replaced Health Bar Crunch as the company's number-one seller. Within the year, virtually every major ice cream company in America was making a cookie dough flavor.

At the time, Ben & Jerry's was already famous for their "What's the Doughboy Afraid of?" campaign against competitor Haagen-Dazs' owner Pillsbury and their equally wacky practice of giving 7.5 percent of pretax profits to charity, but co-owner Jerry Greenfield has said that cookie dough ice cream is what made Ben & Jerry's a financial success.

The flavor was the "invention" of an anonymous customer who scribbled "cookie dough ice cream" on a big pad of paper that hung on the wall of Ben & Jerry's original Burlington, Vermont, ice cream shop in 1984. (I will pause now to give all you business owners time to rustle through those dusty suggestion boxes.)

Deciding it was worth a try, one of the shop's ice cream makers chopped a pan of frozen cookie dough into little cubes and tossed it into chocolate chip ice cream. The result sold so well that customers of nearby Ben & Jerry's stores began demanding it. When the company moved to a new factory in Waterbury the next year, company CEO Fred "Chico" Lager made getting chocolate chip cookie dough into pints a research and development priority/nightmare.

Ice cream add-ins up to that point had either been hard, like a chocolate chip, or soft, like a strawberry. The company had previously figured out how to get Oreos through their so-called "fruit feeders" without clogging to make Oreo Mint, but the sticky cookie dough was more of a problem, Lager recalled a few years later in his book, *Ben & Jerry's: The Inside Scoop.*

After nearly five years of fruitless experiments, Ben & Jerry's consulted Ted Castle, the owner of local commercial baker Rhino Foods. A former All-American hockey player at the University of Vermont, Castle suggested shaping the dough into tiny hockey pucks and shooting them into the ice cream. Using that basic idea, the company was finally able to put the flavor in pints. Chocolate Chip Cookie Dough made with Rhino dough is still among Ben & Jerry's highest scorers, so to speak—being one of only three flavors popular enough to be sold in pints, quarts, mini cups, and at scoop shops.

The original Ben & Jerry's Cookie Dough pint

Never Mind Education and the Economy: Can Their Wives Bake Chocolate Chip Cookies?

Family Circle magazine's Presidential Cookie Bake-Off began as a lighthearted response to Hillary Clinton's infamous 1992 presidential campaign putdown of stay-at-home moms: "I suppose I could have stayed home and baked cookies and had teas, but what I decided to do is fulfill my profession," she had snapped, in answer to a reporter's question about her work for the politically connected Rose Law Firm.

Eager to make amends, Clinton gladly handed over her chocolate chip oatmeal cookie recipe when *Family Circle* called, along with the heartwarming story of baking them every Christmas Eve since she was a child. In their battle against First Lady Barbara Bush's Toll House clone, Hillary's cookies won a greater percentage of the vote than Bill did in his non-cookie contest with George H. W. Bush (55.2 percent versus her husband's 43 percent).

The once-every-four-year contest, where the potential first ladies' recipes are published, tried and voted on by women across the country, has gone on to become the edible Ohio of presidential politics: That state has picked the future sitting president every time but once, and only once in 20 years has the *Family Circle* contest winner not ended up baking her chocolate chip cookie riff in the White House. That was in 2008, the first time in this cookie contest's history when neither of the competitive recipes was some kind of chocolate chip variation.

Coincidence? I think not.

In light of that, it's easy to understand why, for the cookie election of 2012, Michelle Obama ditched her loser 2008 shortbread cookie recipe in favor of a Toll House® recipe variation with extra butter and three kinds of chips.

Hillary Clinton serving cookies

Hillary Clinton's Cookies

This first and still the most popular of *Family Circle*'s presidential cookie contest recipes ranked number one in "overall sensual quality" in a *Consumer Reports* October 1993 survey of 35 fresh-made and packaged chocolate chip cookies.

1½ cups unsifted all-purpose flour
1 teaspoon salt
1 teaspoon baking soda
1 cup solid vegetable shortening
1 cup firmly packed light brown sugar
½ cup granulated sugar
1 teaspoon vanilla extract
2 large eggs
2 cups old-fashioned rolled oats
2 cups (12 ounces) semisweet chocolate chips

Preheat the oven to 350 degrees. Combine the flour, salt, and baking soda. Beat together the shortening, brown sugar, granulated sugar, and vanilla until creamy. Add the eggs, beating until light and fluffy. Gradually beat in the flour mixture and rolled oats. Stir in the chocolate chips. Drop the batter by well-rounded teaspoonfuls onto baking sheets. Bake for 8 to 10 minutes or until the cookies are done. Let the cookies cool on the baking sheets for 2 minutes before placing them on a wire rack for further cooling.

Yield: 90 cookies

Are people at the dawn of the second decade of the 21st century too busy to even bake their baked goods? That might sound plausible (especially to you speed-readers), but it doesn't explain all the cyberspace recipes to make *baked* goods featuring *unbaked* chocolate chip cookie dough, crazy-sounding dishes like cookie dough fudge, cinnamon rolls stuffed with cookie dough, and chocolate chip cookie–stuffed pies. I blame these on a moment in time when the popularity of food blogs on the overstuffed Internet (where only weird ideas stand out and go viral) intersected with the widespread acceptance and use of refrigerated cookie dough as an alternative to making your own, thus making trying these weird cookie-dough treats less of a risk. If Cheez Doodle–stuffed chocolate chip cookies made with refrigerated dough don't taste all that great, well it's not like you put out a lot of time or money to make them.

The eggs in supermarket cookie dough are also pasteurized and the flour in Nestlé's® at least (since 2009) is heat-treated, thus making it less of a medical risk to use in recipes where it isn't cooked much, if at all.

In 2012, these chocolate chip cookie dough recipes even got their own single-subject cookbook.

Yes, in its 75th year, baked or raw, the chocolate chip cookie reigns supreme.

DIY Chocolate Chip Cookie Dough Ice Cream

I'm not sure why you'd want to make your own chocolate chip cookie dough ice cream when Ben & Jerry's and other quality brands of it are readily available at every supermarket and convenience store in the country. But for those who do, here you are.

4 cups light cream
1½ cups sugar
2 cups heavy cream
2 tablespoons vanilla extract
1½ cups No-Cook Cookie Dough, refrigerated until stiff, or
  1 (16.5-ounce) package Nestlé® Toll House® Chocolate Chip Cookie Dough Bar, cut into ½-inch pieces

In a medium saucepan over medium heat, blend the light cream and sugar until the sugar dissolves. Let cool and then stir in the heavy cream and vanilla. Chill for 1 hour before putting into an ice cream machine and freezing according to the manufacturer's directions. When the ice cream is quite stiff, but not yet done, add the cookie dough pieces.

Yield: 2 quarts

No-Cook Cookie Dough

Sure, raw cookie dough is great, but it's not worth a trip to the hospital, or worse. So make your favorite chocolate chip cookie recipe with pasteurized eggs or egg substitute. Or make the below recipe, which is designed to be eaten unbaked and only unbaked—the lack of leavener will make any cookies baked from this as flat as the voices of early-season *American Idol* contestants.

½ cup (1 stick) unsalted butter, softened
¾ cup packed brown sugar
1 tablespoon vanilla extract
⅛ teaspoon salt
1 cup all-purpose flour
1 to 2 tablespoons milk
1 cup mini semisweet chocolate chips

In a medium bowl, cream together the butter and sugar. Mix in the vanilla and salt. Gradually blend in the flour. Add the milk slowly until the mixture reaches a cookie dough consistency. Stir in the chocolate chips. Eat immediately or use in ice cream or another no-bake dessert. Placed in an airtight container, the dough can be frozen for weeks or stored in the refrigerator for about 3 days.

Yield: About 1½ cups

How the Cookies Stack Up

As I said at the beginning of this book, I've (almost) never met a chocolate chip cookie I didn't like. That makes me a poor candidate for rating them. Other, more impartial people have already done that anyway. What follows are the results of some published rankings of chocolate chip cookie products (most recent first); followed by recent sales information for supermarket packaged and cookie dough or how people are voting with their pocketbooks.

2011, *Consumer Reports.* Tate's Bake Shop was the only cookie rated excellent. Among fast-food cookies, McDonald's cookies were judged almost as good as Starbucks' much-pricier ones.

2010, *St. Petersburg Times.* Krusteaz ranked high in this survey of eight boxed chocolate chip cookie mixes.

"Excellent," says *Consumer Reports.*

2009, *Consumer Reports.* Health Valley Minis and Keebler Chips Deluxe Original were deemed the best of 13 supermarket packaged cookies.

2007, *Consumer Reports.* "Close to . . . scratch," the magazine raved about Trader Joe's bags of frozen dough balls in their ranking of supermarket cookie doughs. At 22 cents per cookie, it was also named a best buy.

2006, *Every Day with Rachel Ray.* Tate's and Brent & Sam's Chocolate Chip Pecan were the favorite supermarket brands; Famous 4th Street Cookie Company of Philadelphia (see page 110) got best chewy.

2006, *Washingtonian.* Panera Bread got best from a national chain. They also liked Zabar's and Eleni's (for online), Keebler Chips Deluxe (packaged supermarket) and Brent & Sam's (gourmet packaged supermarket).

2005, *Real Simple*. 600 lb. Gorillas frozen, Pillsbury Chocolate Chunk (now called Chocolate Chunk and Chip), and Nestlé® Toll House Ultimates Chocolate Chip Lovers were preferred, in that order, in this survey of 20 ready-to-bake doughs.

2003, *Good Housekeeping.* Nestlé Toll House Ultimates Chocolate Chip Lovers beat homemade in this supermarket cookie dough survey. Pillsbury Big Classics was runner-up.

1993, *Consumer Reports.* Hillary Clinton's oatmeal–chocolate chip and Nestlé Toll House recipes made from scratch not surprisingly beat out all supermarket mixes and refrigerated doughs. President's Choice and Pepperidge Farm American Collection Nantucket were the top-ranked packaged cookies.

As for what people are actually buying: Among supermarket brands, Nabisco's Chips Ahoy is by far America's favorite, selling about six times the volume of rival Keebler Chips Deluxe, judging from scanner data gathered by SymphonyIRI, a Chicago-based market research firm. If you include all their sub-lines, Pillsbury sells about 25 percent more refrigerated cookie dough than Nestlé Toll House. Frozen dough products (from Otis Spunkmeyer, 600 1b. Gorillas and other companies) currently constitute less than 1 percent of chocolate chip cookies sold in supermarkets, although volume sales in this category almost doubled in the past year.

Rachel Ray faves Brent & Sam's

Stuff It!

This is not a chocolate chip cookie dough book; still, I feel I would be remiss not to tell you about most popular turducken-like chocolate chip cookie/cookie dough dishes.

Cookie Dough–Stuffed Cupcakes: Nestlé® first published a recipe for this back in 2007. After filling cupcake tins with your favorite homemade or cake-mix cake batter, push 1-inch cookie dough balls through the batter to the bottom of the tin. Bake as usual. To really gild the lily, frost the cupcakes with cookie dough frosting (recipe opposite).

Cookie-Stuffed Chocolate Chip Cookies: Jenny Flake (who should really be working with pie crust) posted the cookie-stuffed chocolate chip cookie idea on her Picky Palate blog in January 2011, but Adam Kuban gave it wide visibility a month later on the Serious Eats website. To make, place ice cream-scoop-sized balls of cookie dough on either side of an already baked 2-inch cookie and mash the dough together so that the dough is completely covering the cookie. The original recipe called for Double Stuf Oreos but really, any cookie (Tate's, Chips Ahoy) or candy (Snickers, the possibly redundant Cookie Dough Bites—see page 80) will work. This is the most fun if you completely encase the surprise ingredient in the dough and then serve the baked result to people who just think they're about to eat a regular chocolate chip cookie.

Cookie-Dough-Stuffed Cupcakes

Pookies: Jessie Oleson (aka CakeSpy) may not have pioneered cookie dough cookery, but she seems to be having the most fun with it. Her "pookie" is a pie encased in a chocolate chip cookie. Basically you take an already-baked double-crusted 8-inch fruit pie, completely cover it in cookie dough, put it in a well-greased 10-inch pie plate and bake for 40 or 50 minutes, or until the cookie seems baked. Oleson also makes cookie cake pie, which will only seem weirder than a pookie to people who've never heard of Toll House pie (if so, see page 143), which she's basically baked inside a cake and then frosted. Read on for more precise instructions and the aforementioned cookie dough frosting recipe (to frost it with).

Cookie Cake Pie

1 9-inch (4-cup volume) deep-dish pie shell, unbaked (frozen, refrigerated, or homemade)

1 (16.5-ounce) package refrigerated chocolate chip cookie dough or ½ recipe Original Nestlé® Toll House® Chocolate Chip Cookies (page 123), unbaked, room temperature

½ recipe Toll House Layer Cake (page 152), unbaked

Cookie Dough Frosting

½ cup (1 stick) unsalted butter, softened, or shortening

⅓ cup packed brown sugar

1 teaspoon vanilla extract

½ teaspoon salt

3½ cups confectioners' sugar

4 to 6 tablespoons half-and-half or milk

12 small store-bought chocolate chip cookies, such as Famous Amos (optional)

Mini chocolate chips (optional)

Cookie Cake Pie with Cookie Dough Frosting

For the cookie cake pie: Line a 9-inch pie plate with the pie dough. Place pieces of the cookie dough inside the pie crust and then, using your fingers or a spoon, spread a ½-inch layer of the cookie dough evenly inside the crust. Preheat the oven to 350 degrees. Pour the cake batter on top of the cookie dough until the pie crust is about two-thirds filled. (You may have some cake batter left over.) Bake until a toothpick or cake tester inserted in the center comes out clean, about 35 minutes, then continue to bake for 10 more minutes. The surface of the cake should be uniformly golden. Wrap the perimeter of the pie in foil if the crust gets too dark. Let cool completely. (The pie may crack or fall as it cools but you will cover this up with the icing.)

For the cookie dough frosting: In a large bowl, whip the butter until light and fluffy. Stir in the brown sugar, vanilla, and salt and beat well. Gradually add the confectioners' sugar. Add as much half-and-half as necessary to make the frosting spreadable. Spread the icing on the cooled cookie cake pie, then decorate with the cookies and mini chocolate chips, if desired.

Yield: 8 to 10 servings

4

Chocolate Chips to Go

Chocolate chip cookies are sold at virtually every bakery, coffee shop, supermarket and convenience store in America as well as many restaurants. Listing all of them would be like trying to print out the Internet. This chapter is an attempt (and only an attempt) to identify some places famed for their chocolate chip cookies or chocolate chip cookie dessert spinoffs, with an admitted bias for larger cities versus small, and local venues versus chains (egregious omissions to be gladly incorporated into future editions).

Famous 4th St. Cookie Co.

Arizona

Phoenix

Chelsea's Kitchen, 5040 N. 40th St., 602-957-2555, www.chelseaskitchenaz.com. Even those lukewarm on the other food at this restaurant power spot love the complimentary end-of-meal chocolate chip cookie with sea salt.

Oregano's, numerous Arizona locations, www.oreganos.com. The "pizookie," or pizza cookie was reportedly invented by the BJ's Pizza chain in southern California in the late 1970s but the dessert really caught on in Phoenix, where Oregano's half-pound of cookie dough slightly warmed in a 6-inch pizza pan and topped with three scoops of vanilla bean ice cream is the pizza cookie standard-bearer.

Urban Cookies, 4711 N. 7th St., 602-451-4335, www.urbancookies.com. This shop uses local and organic ingredients and won "Cupcake Wars" in 2011, but its real focus is right there in the name. The taut cookie menu includes the signature Urban Cookie (with dark chocolate, oats, toasted walnuts and coconut bits) and the Simple Urban (more or less a traditional chocolate chip cookie with milk chocolate).

California

Los Angeles

Bouchon Bakery, 235 N. Canon Dr., Beverly Hills, 310-271-9910, www.bouchonbistro.com. See New York City listing.

Clementine, 1715 Ensley Ave., Westwood, 310-552-1080, www.clementineonline.com. This stylish bakery/café's rightly renowned chocolate chip cookie is thin and chewy with a rich brown sugar flavor.

DeLuscious Cookies + Milk, 829 N. Highland Ave., 323-460-2370, www.delusciouscookies.com. This thin and crunchy chocolate chip cookie to the

Clementine

stars (Renee Zellweger, Reese Witherspoon, and Stephen Spielberg included) itself starred in an episode of HBO's *Entourage* (as Drama's bribe to a security guard). More warehouse bakery than storefront, DeLuscious bakes to order (minimum order, six cookies).

Diddy Riese, 926 Broxton Ave., 310-208-0448, www.diddyriese.com. What these cookies lack in flavor, they more than make up for in value: These 3-inch soft chocolate chip cookies are three for a dollar or $1.75 in a sandwich with your choice of Dreyer's ice cream (which is the way most people eat them). On the downside: the perma-line of cash-strapped UCLA students.

Joan's on Third, 8350 W. 3rd St., 323-655-2285, www.joansonthird.com. The chocolate chip cookies come with a side of serious people-watching at this gourmet café/L.A. institution run by black-clad grandmother Joan McNamara and frequented by the likes of Ruth Reichl, Andre Leon Talley, Alexander Skarsgard, and Kate Bosworth. Chase the cookie with one of Joan's signature marshmallow crème–filled chocolate cupcakes.

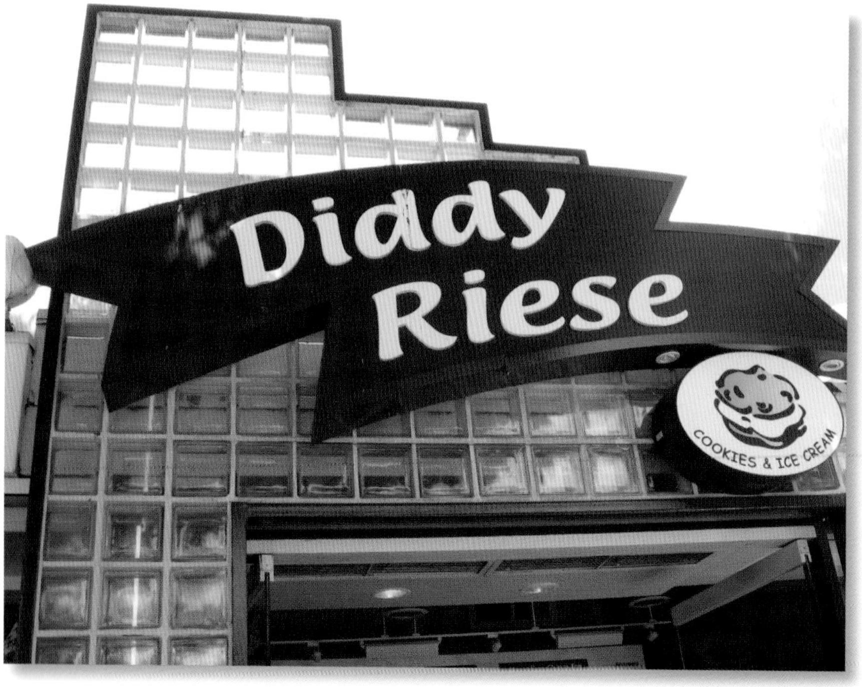

Porto's Bakery & Café, three locations, www.portosbakery.com. Nothing fancy about this bakery or its home-style Toll House®–like chocolate chip cookie, but also nothing not to like (including the price).

Square One, 4854 Fountain Ave., East Hollywood, 323-661-1109, www.squareonedining.com. "It will blow your mind," says L.A. food critic Jonathan Gold of the

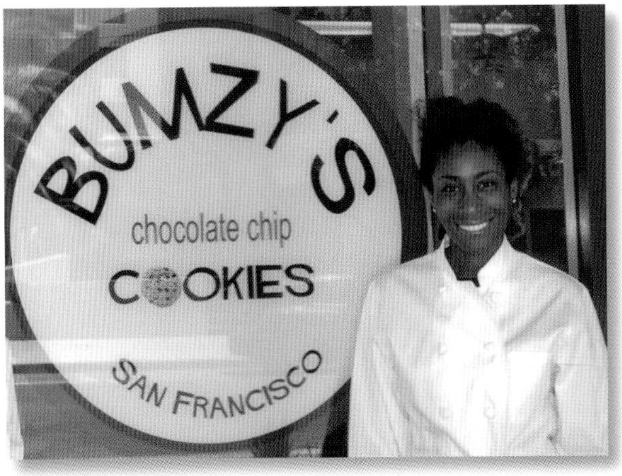

Toni "Bumzy" Young

"enormous, gooey" heavy-on-chocolate chocolate chip cookie served at this trendy breakfast/lunch place.

San Francisco/Bay Area

Bumzy's Chocolate Chip Cookies, 1460 Fillmore St., San Francisco, 415-346-3222, www.bumzyscookies.com. Bumzy has gone commercial with her family's 30-year-old chocolate chip cookie recipe but the customers get treated like family.

The Cookie Department, sold in various Bay area coffee shops and gyms, www.thecookiedepartment.com. Can a chocolate chip cookie be sexy? It can if it contains maca, a purported aphrodisiac, like this cookie company's Chocolate Chip Nookie.

Goody Goodie Cream & Sugar, 1830 Harrison St., San Francisco, 415-864-6370, www.goodygoodie.com. This Mission District dessert salon and café's Old School without nuts was named best chocolate chip cookie in the city by *San Francisco Weekly* in 2010. The signature namesake Goody Goodie boasts a chocolate-to-dough ratio of 4 to 1 from four types of chocolate. The Circus features candied popcorn and chocolate.

Mr. and Mrs. Miscellaneous, 699 22nd St., San Francisco, 415-970-0750. Mainly an ice cream shop but the "miscellaneous" includes a much-praised organic chocolate chip cookie (sometimes with basil or dried cherry add-ins).

Tartine, 600 Guerrero St. (at 18th St.), San Francisco, 415-487-2600, www.tartinebakery.com. Co-owners Elisabeth Prueitt and Chad Robertson shared the 2008 James Beard award for best pastry chef so expect a half-hour wait in line minimum whenever you go to this Mission District temple of sweets and bread. The chocolate chip cookies are saltine-thin, DVD- sized and speckled with nuts, oats, Valrhona chocolate and cacao nibs.

Caramel Corn Chocolate Chip Nestlé® Toll House® Cookies

A Nestlé Kitchens–tested recipe to produce something similar to San Francisco bakery Goody Goodie's Circus creation. Fans of Chicago cookie-maker Bake's pretzel chocolate chip cookie may want to try that variation.

2¼ cups all-purpose flour
1 teaspoon baking soda
1 teaspoon salt
1 cup (2 sticks) butter, softened
¾ cup granulated sugar
¾ cup packed brown sugar
1 teaspoon vanilla extract
2 large eggs
2 cups coarsely chopped caramel popcorn
1 cup (6 ounces) Nestlé Toll House Semi-Sweet Chocolate Morsels
1 cup (6 ounces) Nestlé Toll House Butterscotch or Dark Chocolate Flavored Morsels
1 cup peanuts (plain, or, if you're using the dark chocolate, candied or honey-roasted)

Preheat the oven to 375 degrees. Combine the flour, baking soda, and salt in a small bowl. Using an electric mixer, beat the butter, granulated sugar, brown sugar, and vanilla extract in a large bowl until creamy. Add the eggs, one at a time, beating well after each addition. Gradually beat in the flour mixture. Stir in the popcorn, morsels, and peanuts. Drop by rounded tablespoonfuls onto ungreased baking sheets. Bake for 10 to 12 minutes or until golden brown. Let cool on baking sheets for 2 minutes; remove to wire racks to cool completely.

Yield: 60 cookies

Variation: Omit the butterscotch chips and peanuts. Use 2 cups semisweet chocolate chips and substitute 2 cups small pretzel twists or chocolate-covered pretzel twists (broken into ½-inch pieces) for the caramel popcorn. Bake for 9 to 11 minutes.

Colorado

Denver

Santa Fe Cookie Company, 303 16th St., 303-623-0919. Fresh-baked cookies and trust are served up daily at this downtown self-service cookie bar, which operates on the honor system (pick up your prepacked bag of three cookies and stuff your dollar in the jug).

District of Columbia

Captain Cookie and the Milk Man, various locations, 202-556-3396, www.captaincookiedc.com. Sugar craving threatening to bring our government to a grinding halt? It's this cookie truck to the rescue with a classic chocolate chip, vegan chocolate chip and five choices of milk.

Firehook Bakery, multiple locations in D.C. and Virginia, www.firehook.com. Local bakery/café chain with value-priced 3-inch chocolate chip cookies. With a nod to their environs, they also make a Presidential Sweet oatmeal cookie (fit for one, with its rich chocolate chips, dried cherries, pecans, and coconut ingredients), and iced elephant- and donkey-shaped cookies at election time and by special order.

Captain Cookie and the Milk Man truck

United States of Chocolate Chip Cookies

Chocolate chip cookies are sold all over America but the kind that sells best depends on where you are. As someone who once sold cookies in hundreds of stores all around the country, Debbi Fields is well acquainted with regional preferences. She says chocolate chip cookies with semisweet chocolate do well on the East Coast but that cookie lovers in the candy bar capital of Utah, where Mrs. Fields used to have its headquarters, prefer candy bar–like milk chocolate. As for nuts, walnuts do well on both coasts, Southerners love pecans, and Hawaiians go for the homegrown macadamia (although Fields helped make this nut popular with lots of other people as well).

Grassroots Gourmet, 104 Rhode Island Ave. NW, 202-629-2040, www.grassrootsgourmet.org. Tired of seeing fellow progressives' ideas about community-based business and fair trade fly out the window at the first sign of an Au Bon Pain, Sara Fatell began this to-order bakery delivery business. Her signature Kathy's chocolate chip cookies made with three types of chips contain as much chocolate as dough. A $20 order of two dozen includes a charitable donation and so also that priceless self-righteous feeling.

Marvelous Market, multiple locations, www.marvelousmarket.com. Winner of an exhaustive chocolate chip cookie survey conducted by The *Washingtonian* in 2006 in tribute to its then–recently deceased chocolate chip cookie–loving publisher.

Uncle Chip's Cookie & Dessert Suppliers, 1514 N. Capitol St., 202-999-4990, www.unclechips.com. The egg-averse Shannon Boyle has figured out a way to make a tasty, moist and chewy chocolate chip cookie without eggs. Her bakery/single-item online mail order business is named after Boyle's chocolate chip cookie–loving Uncle Chip.

Florida

Miami

Ali's Sweet Treats, 7094 SW 117 Ave., 305-279-7944, www.alissweettreats.com. Andrea Bernal-Lalun's failed search to find a local source of Elmo-decorated cookies for her daughter Ali's second birthday resulted in what some believe to be Miami's best source of regular and gluten-free chocolate chip cookies (not to mention cupcakes and Elmo cookies).

Hot Cookies, 7545 N. Kendall Dr., 305-666-7777, www.hotcookies.com. One of few shops to serve both chewy and crispy cookies. Mini chocolate chip crispies scooped out of a big popcorn warmer box.

Sweetness Bakeshop and Café, 9549 Sunset Dr., 305-271-7791, www.sweetnessbakeshop.net. Immodestly named Greatest Of All Time (GOAT) chocolate chip cookie is stuffed with chocolate ganache and served warm at this *Miami New Times* Award–winning shop, and by their roaming Sugar Rush dessert truck.

The D.C. YWCA Cookie

Although probably better known for its free museums and spendthrift politicians, Washington, D.C. was also the home of the most-missed chocolate chip cookie in the country. It was sold in, of all places, a YWCA. Located at 17th and K streets, this Y had a cafeteria and a bakery and beginning in the mid-1940s was popular with government drones and bureaucrats who stood in a line that would sometimes stretch out the door and down the block, buying as many as 1,200 cookies per day. At least, that's one way to explain federal government inefficiency until 1981, when the Y moved to a building without a commercial kitchen.

More than 30 years after the last crumb was consumed, the memory of those crisp and chewy, large as saucers, chocolate- and pecan-oozing wonders is still very much alive, judging from the number of Internet postings begging for the recipe.

That recipe was never published. The following is my adaptation of fan Carol Finkelstein's attempt to re-create the cookie that was published in the *Washington Post* in 1977 to raves. In fact, half the people who tried it beside the real Y cookie with food writer Marian Burros at the time said they liked it better.

1⅓ cups unsifted all-purpose flour
1 teaspoon baking soda
¼ teaspoon salt
¼ cup (½ stick) butter
¼ cup solid vegetable shortening
½ cup granulated sugar
¼ cup packed dark brown sugar
1 teaspoon vanilla extract
1 large egg
½ cup coarsely chopped pecans
¼ cup sweetened flaked coconut
¼ cup chocolate chips

Adjust an oven rack to the lowest position and preheat the oven to 375 degrees. Grease two baking sheets. Whisk together the flour, baking soda, and salt. In a large bowl, cream together the butter, shortening, granulated sugar, and brown sugar. Beat in the egg and vanilla. Blend the flour mixture into the wet ingredients. Mix in the walnuts, coconut, and chocolate chips. Divide the dough into 12 equal pieces and place 6 pieces on each baking sheet. Flatten each piece into a 3 1/2-inch round. Bake the cookies, one pan at a time, for 15 minutes. (Even if the cookies look underbaked, take them out.) Let cool on the baking sheet for 2 minutes, then transfer to wire racks to finish cooling.

Yield: 12 cookies

Georgia

Atlanta

Ali's Cookies, Market Plaza Shopping Center, 1255 Johnson Ferry Rd., Marietta, 770-971-8566, www.shipacookie.com. Ali Rosengarten's 100 percent kosher cookies include regular and "house special" chocolate chip (featuring chocolate chips and chunks, oatmeal, and pecans); her Choco Choco Chunks were immortalized on *Rachael Ray*.

Cookie Studio chocolate chips

Alon's, various locations, www.alons.com. Gourmet market with a much-loved decadent pecan chocolate chip cookie.

The Cookie Studio, 30 Pharr Rd., Atlanta, 404-373-8527, www.thecookiestudio.net. Indulge in owner Barbara O'Neill's eight-months-in-the-testing chocolate chip cookie guilt-free since a portion of the proceeds benefits a women's shelter.

Shorty's Pizza, two locations, www.shortys-pizza.com. Pizza place where the dessert favorite is two warm chocolate chip cookies topped with whipped cream.

Savannah

Back in the Day Bakery, 2403 Bull St., 912-495-9292, www.backinthedaybakery.com. Cute as a button retro bakery/café famed for its cupcakes, banana pudding, Drunk Blondies (blondies spiked with bourbon), and, of course, chocolate chip cookies.

Illinois

Chicago

Al's Deli, 914 Noyes St., Evanston, 847-475-9400, www.alsdeli.net. Francophile luncheonette with chocolate chip cookies so popular that there is a four-cookie-per-customer daily limit.

Bake, 2246 W. North Ave., 773-384-7655, www.getbakedchicago.com. Classic American dessert bakery with a saucer-sized soft-and-gooey chocolate chip cookie. A pretzel-containing variation is also much praised.

Cookie Bar, 2475 N. Lincoln Ave., 773-348-0300, www.cookiebaronline.com. THE Chicago bar for people who like sweets as much as liquor. Among the 18 cookie varieties served in '70s-decorated splendor are classic chocolate chip as well as Nutella, jalapeño, potato chip, vegan, and gluten-free variations. Plan your week's cookie eating with their handy online cookie calendar.

Sweet Mandy B's, 1208 W. Webster Ave., 773-244-1174, www.sweetmandybs.com. Classic chocolate chip and chocolate chip cookie sandwiches (with buttercream frosting) sold fresh daily by this sugar-plum-fairy's idea of a bakery named after the owner's kiddies.

Indiana

Indianapolis

Shapiro's Deli, three locations, www.shapiros.com. Century-plus-old classic Jewish deli business whose over-sized desserts include a much-admired chocolate chip cookie, containing both chunks and chips.

Kentucky

Louisville

Brown Hotel, 335 W. Broadway, Louisville, 502-583-1234, www.brownhotel.com. The most famous of about two dozen Louisville restaurants that serve the original Derby Pie, the Kerby family's Southern cousin to the Toll House® pie. (See page 143.) Make sure to precede it with a Hot Brown, the Kentucky-staple open-face hot turkey sandwich invented here.

Maine

Isamax Snacks, various retail locations, 877-447-2629, www.wickedwhoopies.com. Thanks to Oprah, Amy Bouchard's bakery (named after her kids Isabella and Max) is one of the most famous sources of whoopie pies in the country. Isamax is important to us for its chocolate chip cookie–flavored whoopie.

Maine Diner, 2265 Post Rd., Wells, 207-646-4441, www.mainediner.com. Go for

John Kerry and the Cookie Entrepreneur Veteran for Truth

When talking about small business in his election campaigns for U.S. Senate and the presidency, now–Secretary of State John Kerry regularly trotted out his experience as the founding co-owner of Boston cookie stand Kilvert & Forbes.

It was in 1976: Kerry was practicing law, which he found "quite predictable and very boring." A big chocolate chip cookie fan, he got the idea of selling cookies from family recipes with friend and longtime political operative K. Dun Gifford. The shop's name came from combining the maiden names of their mothers. Kerry says he would occasionally whip up a batch of the shop brownies until his political career took off and he sold out in the mid-1980s. But the experience gave him a long-lasting appreciation for what small businesspeople are up against, yada yada.

But fellow cookie entrepreneur David Liederman says what the cookie stand really gave John Kerry was a chance to rip him off.

Liederman says Kerry called him up one day in 1979 or 1980 and asked to meet about opening a David's Cookies store in Boston. "So I gave him the layout, the package, and he went back and I didn't hear from him for six or seven months." Then Liederman got a call from someone who said he'd seen a David's Cookies at Faneuil Hall in Boston. Not having a Boston shop, Liederman decided to go up and take a look. The Kilvert & Forbes shop was, according to Liederman, "a direct, 100-percent knock-off of David's Cookies," from the design to the appliances to the cookies. When he called Kerry to point this out, Liederman said Kerry replied, "You're absolutely right. I am a politician; I shouldn't be in the cookie business, so let me sell you my store."

Liederman declined because, outrageousness of the idea of buying his own business aside, Kerry was operating in violation of his lease. "He was supposed to be selling jams and jellies, not cookies," Liederman wrote in his business biography, *Running Through Walls*, and has been repeating, at the behest of Kerry's political opponents, ever since.

Nevertheless Liederman voted for Kerry for president in 2004. "I'd support anybody that wasn't Bush . . . although Bush never stole David's Cookies from me," he told a reporter at the time.

their Toll House® pie–like chocolate chip cookie dough pie–but I could be rightly sued for food-writing malpractice if I didn't also mention their signature New England lobster roll and pie, and Indian and Grape-Nut puddings (among this place's embarrassment of Down East culinary riches).

Marnee's Cookie Bistro, 906 High St., Bath, 207-443-3401, www.marnees.com. Their nationally renowned signature Nirvana is an aptly named chewy-crunchy chocolate chip cookie with oats, toffee, and honey.

Maryland

Otterbein's, various local grocery and gourmet food stores, 410-265-8700, www.otterbeinsbakery.com. Otterbein's all-natural, thin and crispy sugar cookies are a 132-year-old tradition in Baltimore. Their chocolate chip cookies are something like Tate's (see New York listing and page 108).

Massachusetts

Boston

The Chipyard, 257 Faneuil Hall, 617-742-9537, www.chipyard.com. This lone survivor of a 1970s cookie chain sells bags of warm, bite-sized cookies to tourists and locals in historic Faneuil Hall.

Clear Flour, 178 Thorndike St., Brookline, 617-739-0060, www.clearflourbread.com. Hidden away on the bottom shelf of a baking rack in this tiny artisan-style bread bakery is what *Boston Magazine* has dubbed Boston's best chocolate chip

Clear Flour's award-winner

cookie, for good reason: It's multi-textured, not too sweet, and infused with serious European chocolate.

Flour, three locations, www.flourbakery.com. Joanne Chang bailed on the lucrative management-consultant track laid out by her Harvard applied math and economics degree to make these flat but complex, TCHO chocolate–containing chocolate chip cookies (and possibly even more revered sticky buns, banana bread, and toaster pastries).

How Can They Make Chocolate Chip Cookies All Day and Not Be Blimps?

Carol Goldman of Carol's Cookies in Chicago and Judy Rosenberg of *Rosie's Bakery Chocolate-Packed, Jam-Filled, Butter-Rich, No-Holds-Barred Cookie Book* fame have both been serious runners. And Levain Bakery co-owners Connie McDonald and Pamela Weekes met while training for Ironman competitions.

Kilvert & Forbes/Maggie's Sweets, 200 Faneuil Hall, 617-723-6050, www.kilvertandforbesbakeshop.com. The cookie shop started by a young John Kerry is still going strong, selling enormous soft chocolate chip cookies under a sign with a cartoony typeface that still looks like David's. (See "John Kerry and the Cookie Entrepreneur Veteran for Truth," page 98.)

Rosie's Bakery, four locations, www.rosiesbakery.com. Boston baking institution Judy "Rosie" Rosenberg (she of the IACP and Best of Boston awards and multiple cookbooks) sells 57,000 of her old-fashioned flat 4-inch chocolate chip cookies annually.

Rosie's Bakery case

Volle Nolle, 351 Hanover St., 617-523-0003. The sweet-and-salty chocolate chip cookie is the only baked good offered at this small restaurant. It's so good, nothing else is necessary.

Martha's Vineyard

State Road, 688 State Rd., West Tisbury, 508-693-8582, www.stateroadmv.com. Ed Levine of *Serious Eats* calls the pliant chocolate chip cookies at this restaurant-bakery-café "miniature masterpieces" of insane flavor.

Michigan

Detroit

Astoria Pastry Shop, two locations, 313-963-9603, www.astoriapastryshop.com. Traditional Greek Bakery known for its Michigan chocolate chunk cookie (featuring Michigan cherries).

Avalon International Breads, 422 W. Willis St., 313-832-0008, www.avalonbreads.net. Believe it or not, artisanal baked goods made with organic flour in the heart of downtown Detroit, including some reportedly truly amazing sea-salt chocolate chip cookies.

Pinwheel Bakery, 220 W 9 Mile Rd., Ferndale, 248-398-8018, www.pinwheelbakery.com. Their vegan chocolate chip cookies got their 15 minutes thanks to an online shout-out from Alicia Silverstone when she was in town to shoot a movie.

Minnesota

Minneapolis/St. Paul

Cookie Cart, 1119 W. Broadway Ave., Minneapolis, 612-521-0855, www.cookiecart.org. Sister Jean Thuerauf's idea for keeping kids out of trouble—by having them bake cookies and sell them from a pushcart—is now a storefront/delivery service and nonprofit organization that still employs and trains teens. The traditional chocolate chip variety is one of eight "cookies with a cause."

Pizzeria Lola, 5557 Xerxes Ave S., Minneapolis, 612-424-8338, www.pizzerialola.com. One of many American pizza places where the ovens do double-duty making superior chocolate chip cookies; in this upscale case, sprinkled with sea salt and served with a "shot" of milk.

Rustica Bakery, 3220 West Lake St., Minneapolis, 612-822-1119, www.rusticabakery.com. Renowned by *Bon Appetit* for their bread, this place also makes sophisticated caramely chocolate chip cookies and fudgy bittersweet chocolate cookies.

Sebastian Joe's, two locations, Minneapolis, www.sebastianjoesicecream.com. An ice creamery that also makes superior DVD-sized chocolate chip cookies. Try two around a slab of their signature Pavarotti (banana-caramel-chocolate) ice cream.

Sweet Martha's Cookie Jar, two stands at the Minnesota State Fair, St. Paul, www.sweetmarthas.com. Buckets of warm Sweet Martha's chocolate chip cookies are an icon of the Minnesota State Fair and now locals can get their Martha's fix the other 353 days of the year via packaged Martha's dough in supermarket freezers.

Tank Goodness, various locations, 612-824-8265, tankgoodness.com. The pun- and fun-loving Tanks family bakes and delivers warm oatmeal chocolate chip cookies (and only oatmeal chocolate chip cookies) to your door via Mini Cooper.

Nevada

Las Vegas

Bouchon Bakery, Venetian Hotel and Casino, 3355 Las Vegas Blvd. S., 702-414-6200, www.bouchonbistro.com. (See New York City listing.)

Grand Lux Café, Venetian Hotel and Casino, 3355 Las Vegas Blvd. S., 702-414-3888, www.grandluxcafe.com. The Cheesecake Factory founder's idea of a Venetian café dessert menu includes a dozen baked-to-order American pecan chocolate chip cookies. (Not that I'm complaining.)

Red Velvet Café, various locations, 702-360-1972, www.theredvelvetcafe.com. Playboy Bunny Holly Madison has tweeted that Cordon Bleu-trained baker Aneesha Tolani's low-cal vegan chocolate chip cookies are "the bomb" and others apparently agree.

New Jersey

Crazy Susan's, locations in Ocean City and Vorhees, www.crazysusanscookies.com. Come meet Food Network *Tough Cookies* show star Susan Adair and try one of her best-selling chocolate chip cookies or specialty Crazy Turtles (chocolate chip cashew cookies slathered with caramel and milk chocolate).

New York

New York City

Amy's Bread, 672 9th Ave., 212-977-2670, www.amysbread.com. Amy Scheiber's shrine to artisanal bread wasn't open a year before customers made it clear that they needed to squeeze a few sheet pans of cookies into the bread ovens. The basic back-of-the-bag chocolate chip cookie recipe eventually evolved into the current "nuevo" one (with the "subtle flavors of . . . toasted wheat, melted butter, and molasses," says Amy).

Baked, 359 Van Brunt St., Brooklyn, 718-222-0345, www.bakednyc.com. Hipster bakery that makes homey desserts with a twist. Can't decide between their great chocolate chip cookie and even-more-famous brownie? Choose the Brookster, their best-selling cupcake-sized brownie-cookie confection that combines the two.

Bouchon Bakery, two NYC locations, www.bouchonbakery.com. Although logic dictates you check out their macaroons and namesake cork-shaped Bouchon brownies, Michelin award-winning chef Thomas Keller's French bakery menu also includes an all-American chocolate chip cookie that *Serious Eats* ranked second only to Tom Cat's.

City Bakery, 3 W. 18th St., 212-366-1414, www.thecitybakery.com. The second most famous chocolate chip cookie in New York City is about 6 chewy inches in diameter and has a distinct baking soda taste. Owner Maury Rubin sells about 1,000 a day. Chocolate lovers might also want to check out their unique pretzel croissant with chocolate dipping sauce.

A stack at City Bakery in New York City

Insomnia Cookies, three Manhattan locations, www.insomniacookies.com. (See Philadelphia listing and side story.)

Jacques Torres Chocolate, various locations, 718-875-1269, www.mrchocolate.com. The supposed basis for the famous *New York Times* "perfect" chocolate chip cookie recipe, chocolate chip cookies sold here would appear to be a shell vehicle for a whole lot of Torres's excellent chocolate.

Levain Bakery, three locations, www.levainbakery.com. The home of one of the two most famous bakery chocolate chip cookies in the country. Mecca for lovers of cakey chocolate chip cookies. (See "Sweet Land of Levain," on page 74.)

Momofuku Milk Bar, various locations, www.milkbarstore.com. "It" pastry chef Christina Tosi's quirky tributes to the chocolate chip cookie include the Compost (a brown sugar dough studded with chocolate chunks, pretzels, potato chips, and coffee grounds) and the Cornflake–Chocolate Chip–Marshmallow. (See "Cornflake-Marshmallow Toll House® Tribute," opposite page.)

Sarabeth's Bakery, Chelsea Market, 75 9th Ave., 212-989-2424, www.sarabeth.com. Clouds are an unusual lacey variation on the basic chocolate chip with sliced almonds. They are the happy result of a worker at this dessert-focused branch of Sarabeth Levine's New York restaurant empire accidentally quadrupling the sugar in a traditional chocolate chip cookie recipe.

Tom Cat Bakery, sold at various coffeehouses around the city, www.tomcatbakery.com, www.roastingplant.com. The *Serious Eats* website's extensive early 2010 survey declared these flavorful, flat chocolate chip cookies the city's best, and the Roasting Plant, which bakes them off in two locations multiple times daily, the best place to buy them. The Rube Goldberg–style roasting contraption that periodically blasts the Plant's beans through tubing around the shop are alone worth the trip.

Treats Truck/Treats Truck Stop, 521 Court St., Brooklyn, 212-691-5226, www.thetreatstruck.com. The crispy-on-the-edges, soft-in-the-middle chocolate chip cookie is a staple of Vendy Award–winning baker Kim Ima's "nothing too fancy, always delicious" menu of mobile treats.

The Hamptons

Levain Bakery, 354 Montauk Highway, Wainscott, 631-537-8570, www.levainbakery.com. (See the Levain Bakery sidebar on page 74.)

Tate's Bake Shop, 43 North Sea Rd., Southampton, 631-283-9830, www.tatesbakeshop.com. The cookies here are pretty much the same as the all-natural crispy Tate's sold in your local gourmet store. Come here instead for the almost

Cornflake-Marshmallow Toll House® Tribute

There is no traditional chocolate chip cookie on Momofuku Milk Bar's menu (there's no traditional *anything* served there actually) and their delicious "chocolate chip tribute cookie—one of our most popular cookies," according to chef/owner Christina Tosi—was created by accident. A fellow chef at sister restaurant Momofuku Ko had overtoasted the cornflake crunch for the cereal milk panna cotta, and instead of throwing it away, Tosi decided to put it in some cookies for the staff meal, along with some chocolate chips and mini marshmallows "in case the cornflakes were a bust." Instead the Ko staff asked for the cornflake-chocolate chip-marshmallow cookies to be served the next night, the night after, and the night after that. This is a simplification of the recipe in Tosi's *Momofuku Milk Bar* cookbook.

4 cups corn flakes cereal
1 cup plus 2 tablespoons granulated sugar, divided
⅓ cup salted butter, melted
1 cup (2 sticks) unsalted butter, room temperature
¾ cup packed light brown sugar
1 large egg
½ teaspoon vanilla extract
1½ cups all-purpose flour
1¼ teaspoons kosher salt
½ teaspoon baking powder
½ teaspoon baking soda
¾ cup mini chocolate chips
1 cup mini marshmallows

Preheat the oven to 275 degrees. Line a baking sheet with parchment paper. Crumble the corn flakes in a bowl with your hands. Add the melted salted butter and 2 tablespoons of the granulated sugar and stir well to combine. Form into clusters and place them evenly on the baking sheet. Bake until the clusters are toasted and fragrant, about 20 minutes. (Turn off the oven.) While the clusters are cooling, beat the unsalted butter, remaining granulated sugar, brown sugar, egg, and vanilla together in a large bowl until creamy (as long as 8 minutes). Combine the flour, salt, powder and soda in another bowl, then add to the creamed mixture in stages just until a dough forms. Gently fold in the corn flake clusters, chocolate chips, and marshmallows. Cover the bowl with plastic wrap and refrigerate for at least 1 hour.

Preheat the oven to 375 degrees. Line two baking sheets with more parchment paper. Place ⅓-cup portions of dough on the sheets at least 4 inches apart and flatten them with your hands into disks. Bake for 18 minutes or until the edges and centers have just started to brown. Let cool completely on the baking sheets.

Yield: 15 to 20 cookies

equally delicious lemon squares, pie, and pound cake; the charming country-cottage setting; and the possibility of running into one of the 21st-century's few true chocolate chip cookie celebrities. (See "The King of Crispy and Thin," page 108.)

Ohio

Cincinnati

Donna's Gourmet Cookies, 10796 Montgomery Rd., 513-489-9600, www.donnasgourmetcookies.com. *Cincinnati Magazine* dubbed Donna Phelps's multi-textured behemoths this city's best.

Oregon

Portland

Alma Chocolate, 140 NE 28th Ave., 503-517-0262, www.almachocolate.com. The dark chocolate shards star, not surprisingly, in this chocolate shop's smallish caramely chocolate chip cookies or, as they call them, OMG Chocolate Chip Cookies.

Courier Coffee Roasters, 923 SW Oak St., 503-545-6444, www.couriercoffeeroasters.com. Coffee roaster and café (called Courier because they deliver their coffee by bike) with a

Tate's Bake Shop

much-praised cookie that contains 72 percent cacao chocolate.

Dovetail Bakery, 3039 NE Alberta St., 503-288-8839, www.dovetailbakery.blogspot.com. If any place could do a good vegan chocolate chip cookie, it would have to be in Portland, right?

Ken's Artisan Bakery, 338 NW 21st Ave., 503-248-2202, www.kensartisan.com. Although best known for his rustic breads and bread-baking book, Ken Forkish also makes a noteworthy saucer-sized Valrhona Caraibe chocolate chip cookie.

Pearl, 102 NW 9th Ave., 503-827-0910, www.pearlbakery.com. Toasted pecans, Mexican vanilla, and orange zest distinguish the chocolate chip cookie at this 15-year-old family-run bakery not far from the famous Powell's bookstore (so you can satisfy your intellectual and sweets cravings at the same time).

The Sugar Cube, 1212 SE Hawthorne Blvd., 503-890-2825, www.sugarcubepdx.com. Kir Jensen chucked the fine-dining pastry track to sell regular and hazelnut-infused chocolate chip cookies (see "Twisted Toll House®," page 111)—and many other even fancier things—from a Neapolitan ice cream–colored camper.

Two Tarts, 2309 NW Kearney St., 503-312-9522, www.twotartsbakery.com. It's all about the sea salt they sprinkle on top of their chocolate chip cookies at Two Tarts, a mostly organic, all compostable bakery that got its start at a Portland farmer's market.

Kir Jensen of The Sugar Cube

The King of Crispy and Thin

Kathleen King has lived the dream of every kid who has ever set up a card table by the side of the road and tried to sell something.

In her case, that something was chocolate chip cookies and Famous Amos was her idol. At age 11, manning a baked goods table at her father's Southampton, New York, farm stand, King recalls, "I used to dream of him pulling up in his Cadillac and purple outfit."

King grew up to become Wally Amos's 21st century counterpart, in the sense of being nationally famous for her chocolate chip cookies and also, someone who once lost her cookie business and business name, "just like Famous Amos," she says today with a hearty laugh.

Kathleen King, age 11, with cake

Like most farm kids, King worked from the day she could walk: gathering eggs, cleaning pens, and eventually inheriting the job of baking for her dad's farm stand when her older sister decided "she wanted a real job where there were boys." But where her sister mainly made pies, breads, and brownies, King concentrated on chocolate chip cookies, at first, using the money she made to buy clothes; later to pay for college.

In the early 1980s, she opened Kathleen's Bake Shop in a colonial clapboard building containing large country pine tables piled high with classic American treats—brownies, pies, and her signature thin and crispy chocolate chip cookies. By the mid-'90s, Kathleen's Cookies were also being sold at gourmet and department stores up and down the East Coast.

It was an effort to expand that packaged cookie business that got King into Famous Amos–like money and legal trouble, partnering with a former employee and his brother who, according to newspaper accounts at the time, changed her recipe, got behind on bills, moved manufacturing to Virginia, and, amidst arguments with her about all this, in January 2000, fired King from her own business. For the next few months friends and relatives picketed the bake shop, carrying signs reading, "WHAT HAPPENED TO KATHLEEN?" and "NO KATHLEEN, NO COOKIES." That July, King and her former partners reached a legal agreement where she lost the legal right to use her name in a bakery business but reclaimed the shop, though she had to take out a loan to reopen. And she had to do it fast, before the last four weeks of the lucrative Long Island tourist season passed.

What happened next resembles the last act of the movie *It's a Wonderful Life*. Her first call was to a local sign maker: In 10 minutes he was there with a banner saying she was reopening as Tate's (a nickname her farmer dad attained while picking 'taters as a boy). Other tradespeople worked on the bakery gratis. Creditors called and wished her well, telling her to pay them whenever she could. A thousand people showed up for the open house, another 700 on opening day,

Kathleen King today with cookie dough

forming a line that stretched down the street. "All these people . . . turned an ugly situation into a positive thing," she told a newspaper reporter at the time.

Five years later, King's business was back to where it was and then some. Her wholesale bakery in East Moriches, New York currently ships out about 65 million cookies a year to stores in almost all 50 states. Fans include *Consumer Reports* and *Every Day with Rachael Ray* (both of which have named Tate's "best chocolate chip cookie") and vacationing celebrities Alan Alda, Billy Joel, Christie Brinkley, and Caroline Kennedy Schlossberg—although King has yet to meet idol/doppelganger Famous Amos.

Copycat Tate's

Like Wally Amos, Kathleen King has always freely shared her chocolate chip cookie recipe. That could be partly because, like Amos, she bases her recipe on the Toll House® one, with a few minor tweaks and top-quality ingredients. Slavish adherence to pan preparation, dough-ball size, and cooking time are key to creating the thin, crispy Tate's-like chocolate chip cookie, which you could easily buy in a gourmet store or online at www.tatesbakeshop.com (a word to the lazy probably being sufficient).

2 cups all-purpose flour
1 teaspoon baking soda
1 teaspoon salt
1 cup (2 sticks) salted butter
¾ cup granulated sugar
¾ cup firmly packed dark brown sugar
1 teaspoon water
1 teaspoon vanilla extract
2 large eggs
2 cups (12 ounces) semisweet chocolate chips

Preheat the oven to 350 degrees. Generously grease two baking sheets. In a medium bowl, mix together the flour, baking soda, and salt. In a large bowl, cream the butter, granulated sugar, and brown sugar, then add the water and vanilla and blend just until combined. Stir the eggs in gently. Fold in the flour mixture, and afterwards, the chocolate chips. Drop 2-tablespoon mounds of dough at least 2 inches apart onto the prepared cookie sheets. Bake for 12 to 17 minutes or until the edges and centers of the cookies are brown. Remove from the oven and allow to cool on wire racks.

Yield: 54 cookies

Pennsylvania

Philadelphia

Ela, 627 S. 3rd St., 267-687-8512, www.elaphilly.com. Hunky high-end restaurant chef Jason Cichonski's equally hot cookie dough dessert is molten chocolate chip cookie batter poured tableside onto vanilla semifreddo slathered with banana–black pepper jam.

Famous 4th Street Cookies, Reading Terminal Market, 51 N. 12th St., 215-922-3274, www.famouscookies.com. This stand in the historic Reading Terminal Market is, in fact, probably the most famous place for cookies in Philly. The cookies are a splinter business of the Famous 4th Street Jewish deli on Fourth Street (hence the name), whose new and different owners nevertheless maintain the old tradition of giving away one of these thick, moist and chewy cookies at the end of every meal.

Hope's Cookies, 1125 W. Lancaster Ave., Rosemont, 610-527-4488, www.hopescookies.com. Hope's is a 27-year tradition on Philly's wealthy suburban Main Line, not far from owner Hope Spivak's alma mater, Bryn Mawr College (whose students, according to one online survey, eat an average of two all-natural Hope's cookies per week).

Philadelphia's Metropolitan Bakery in winter

Insomnia Cookies, two downtown locations, 877-632-6654, www.insomniacookies.com. Two of this college cookie-delivery chain's few stores for the post- or never-went-to-college crowd. Pick-up, eat-in or delivery until 3 am. (See "Late Night with Cookies," page 112.)

Metropolitan Bakery, various locations, www.metropolitanbakery.com. Philly's finest local artisanal bread bakery is also known for

Twisted Toll House® Cookies

Hazelnut flour gives this chocolate chip variation served by Portland's Sugar Cube dessert cart an incredibly nutty flavor, but the oil in that nut makes for a flat and crispy cookie. Chubby-cookie lovers should follow that variation. The recipe is from cart owner Kir Jensen's *The Sugar Cube: 50 Deliciously Twisted Treats from the Sweetest Food Truck on the Planet*. You can buy hazelnut flour from Bob's Red Mill or King Arthur Flour, or make it yourself.

1¾ cups unbleached all-purpose flour
½ cup hazelnut flour
1 teaspoon baking soda
1 teaspoon sea salt
1 cup (2 sticks) unsalted butter, room temperature
¾ cup granulated sugar
¾ cup packed dark brown sugar
2 large eggs, room temperature
1 teaspoon vanilla extract
1¾ to 2 cups (about 10 ounces) finely chopped 70 percent bittersweet chocolate
Fleur de sel for sprinkling

In a medium bowl, whisk together the all-purpose flour, hazelnut flour, baking soda and salt. In the bowl of a stand mixer fitted with the paddle attachment, cream the butter, granulated sugar, and brown sugar on high speed until light and fluffy, about 2 minutes. Add the eggs, one at a time, beating well after each addition. Beat in the vanilla. Scrape down the sides of the bowl. With the mixer on low, add the dry ingredients and beat just until combined. Stir in the chopped chocolate, using the larger amount if you're a chocolate fanatic. Chill the dough for at least 2 hours, or (if you can wait) overnight to give the flavors a chance to mature.

Preheat the oven to 350 degrees. Line two large baking sheets with parchment paper or silicone liners. With a medium ice cream scoop, drop 2-tablespoon portions of dough about 2 inches apart onto the prepared baking sheets.
Bake until golden brown, 12 to 14 minutes, rotating the sheets from front to back and between upper and lower racks after about 10 minutes. Sprinkle the cookies with fleur de sel while still warm and let cool on the baking sheets for a minute before transferring them to a wire rack to cool completely. The cookies will keep in an airtight container for several days.

The Sugar Cube chocolate chip cookies

Yield: 24 cookies.
Variation: To make the cookies thicker and more like a classic Toll House cookie, increase the all-purpose flour to 2 cups, reduce the hazelnut flour to ¼ cup and add ¾ cup chopped lightly toasted hazelnuts. Instead of finely chopped chocolate, use 1¾ to 2 cups dark bittersweet chocolate chips.

Late Night with Cookies

It's 1 am and you're craving chocolate chip cookies. What do you do? (1) Scrounge around to see what you have in the house, (2) go to the local 24-hour convenience store, or (3) if you're lucky enough to live somewhere with an Insomnia Cookies, go to www.insomniacookies.com and place your order for a half-dozen warm ones to be delivered fresh to your door.

University of Pennsylvania junior Seth Berkowitz started Insomnia in 2002 just baking cookies for fellow students in his dorm room and delivering them by bicycle. By 2005, he had trucks or bakeries making cookies for students at Penn, Drexel, Syracuse, the University of Illinois, and the University of Maryland.

Insomnia is not America's first cookie-delivery service or even its first or only student-started college-oriented one (see Tiff's in Texas, for another). But with service at 18 colleges and counting, it's the largest and the most rapidly growing.

Insomnia has recently woken up to the business opportunity in the big cities, opening storefronts with late-night walkup and delivery service for anybody and everybody—because you never outgrow your need for warm cookies and cold milk, especially when you can't sleep.

Insomnia Cookies at night

its big, crunchy, salty, and not-at-all-sour sour cherry chocolate chip cookie. (See recipe on page 114.)

Old City Coffee, 221 Church St., 215-629-9292, www.oldcitycoffee.com. Store-baked cookies and cakes are a match as well as a great accompaniment to their strong, store-roasted coffee. The chocolate chip cookies have a sugary taste and a crumbly shortbread consistency.

Old City Coffee cookie jar

Tartes Fine Cakes & Pastries, 212 Arch St., 215-625-2510. Although best known for their namesake tarts, this pink dollhouse of a walk-up bakery less than a block from where Betsy Ross supposedly invented our flag also sells a tanning salon–gorgeous soft and chewy chocolate chip cookie with pecans.

Rhode Island

Providence

Meeting Street Café, 220 Meeting St., 401-273-1066, www.meetingstreetcafe.com. College Hill restaurant with cookies so big you can buy them by the half.

Seven Stars, two locations, www.sevenstarsbakery.com. Artisanal bakery/café with a chocolate chip cookie appreciated for its sugar restraint.

Tennessee

Memphis

Ricki's Cookie Corner, 5068 Park Ave., 901-866-2447, www.rickiscookiecorner.com. Kosher bakery known for its Chipsticks, mini chocolate chip cookies shaped like half-hermits.

Nashville

Christie Cookie Company, 1205 3rd Ave. N., 615-242-3817, www.christiecookies.com. The cookie company that DoubleTree hotels made famous (and vice versa; see page 186) was in 2001 split into two companies: a chain of five Nashville-area retail cookie and gelato shops run by company founder Christie Hauck, and this one, owned by his former business partner. Although mainly a mail order and food service company, this place does have a factory store where you can buy both the signature DoubleTree cookie and the original Christie cookie (a chocolate chip cookie with Heath Bar pieces).

Christie Cookies and Bravo Gelato, five retail locations, 615-259-4438. Christie Hauck's Christie Cookies started as a retail store in 1983 and it is retail stores—with cookies and gelato and chairs tables—that he runs today. (See above.)

Salted Chocolate Chip and Sour Cherry Cookies

You might not have thought to add cherries to your chocolate chip cookies. But James Barrett of Metropolitan Bakery in Philadelphia did. It is now Metropolitan's most popular cookie, outselling the more straightforward chocolate chip version he also makes.

1 cup old-fashioned rolled oats
3 cups all-purpose flour
1¾ teaspoons baking powder
1½ teaspoons baking soda
1¼ teaspoons kosher salt
1½ cups (3 sticks) unsalted butter, room temperature
1¾ cups packed light brown sugar
1¼ cups granulated sugar
3 large eggs
1½ teaspoons vanilla extract
3½ cups extra bittersweet chocolate chunks
1¼ cups dried tart cherries
4½ teaspoons coarse sea salt

Salted Chocolate Chip and Sour Cherry Cookies

In the bowl of a food processor grind the oats into a fine flour. Sift the all-purpose flour with the baking powder and baking soda. Add the kosher salt and oat flour and set aside. In the bowl of a stand mixer fitted with the paddle attachment, cream together the butter, brown sugar, and granulated sugar until light, approximately 3 minutes.

Add the eggs one at a time. Stir in the vanilla. Add the flour mixture and mix until just combined. Fold in the chocolate and cherries just until incorporated. Using a large ice cream scoop, form the cookie dough into generous ¼-cup (4-ounce) balls. Place the dough balls on a parchment-lined tray. Wrap and chill overnight, or up to 3 days.

Preheat the oven to 350 degrees. Transfer the dough balls to baking sheets, spacing them 2 inches apart. Press slightly to flatten the dough and sprinkle the top of each with ¼ teaspoon coarse sea salt. Bake 15 to 18 minutes, rotating the baking sheets between the upper and lower oven racks halfway through baking, until golden brown around the edges. Transfer the cookies to wire racks and serve warm or let cool completely.

Yield: 18 large cookies

Texas

Austin

Frank, 407 Colorado St., 512-494-6916, www.hotdogscoldbeer.com. High-end hot dog bar where you can also pig out on the Frankencookie, a warm chocolate chip, pecan, walnut, cranberry, and bacon cookie topped with coffee ice cream, sprinkled with candied bacon crumbles, and served with a couple of strips of bacon. (Dieters can ask them to hold the ice cream or bacon, or better yet, eat elsewhere.)

Quack's 43rd St Bakery, 411 E. 43rd St., 512-453-3399, www.quacksbakery.com. Slacker coffee shop/bakery whose Texas-sized chocolate chip cookie is among the top 2 percent of all Austin restaurant dishes praised online, according to website *Dishtip*.

Tiff's Treats, three locations (also in Houston and Dallas), www.cookiedelivery.com. Tiffany Taylor and Leon Chen started baking cookies for fellow University of Texas students out of Chen's college

Leon Chen and Tiffany Taylor Chen of Tiff's Treats

apartment in 1999, and now they're a married couple/Texas cookie juggernaut, delivering chocolate chip and nine other hot, gooey cookies to the general public from nine storefronts in three cities. Pick-up customers can also get Tiffwiches, cookie ice cream sandwiches made with Southern favorite ice cream brand Blue Bell.

Upper Crust Bakery, 4508 Burnet Rd., 512-467-0102, www.theuppercrustbakery.com. This bakery/café has won multiple *Austin Chronicle* Reader's Choice awards and accolades for its crispy chocolate chip with nuts.

Dallas

Crème de la Cookie, various locations, www.cremedelacookie.com. "Caution! May cause extreme drooling resulting in keyboard damage," warns the menu on Crème de la Cookie's website. At least some of this can be attributed to owner Toni Rivard's award-winning OMG Chocolate Chip Cookie, featuring European butter, Schokinag chocolate, and lots of dark brown sugar.

Great One Cookie Company, 3111-B Monticello Ave., 214-219-3111, www.greatonecookies.com. "If you're going to eat a cookie, eat a great one" is Pam Denesuk's philosophy and the name of her company, which aims to provide one great chocolate chip cookie, featuring both milk and semisweet chocolate.

JD's Chippery, 6601 Hillcrest Ave., 214-363-2038, www.jdschippery.com. This place dates back to the early 1980s cookie retail store craze. The D is long gone but John and Julie Broad continue to bake their namesake chocolate chip cookies in small batches six days a week.

Houston

Michael's Cookie Jar, 5330 Weslayan St., 713-771-8603, www.michaelscookiejar.com. CIA-trained chef Michael Savino makes all-natural chocolate chunk cookies (and many other buttery 3-inchers) behind a Petco.

Utah

Salt Lake City

RubySnap, 770 S. 300 West, 801-834-6111, www.rubysnap.com. Frozen cookie dough shop formerly known as Dough Girl (because owner Tami Cromar names her cookies after retro pin-up girls) became nationally known a couple of years ago when the Pillsbury Doughboy's lawyers came calling. Traditional Trudy chocolate chip cookie and best-selling Vivianna variation (featuring dark chocolate, mangos, and a citrus-accented dough) and 10 other cookies are available baked on-site or as frozen dough to take home.

Washington

Seattle

Cinnamon Works, Pike Place Market, 1536 Pike Pl., 206-583-0085, www.cinnamonworks.com. This place started as a cinnamon roll stand in the early 1980s but now features a full line of baked goods, including the best gluten-free chocolate chip cookie in the city, according to many.

Cow Chip Cookies, two locations, www.cowchipcookies.com. Has overcome an association with dried cow dung (and bad farm puns) with what some online posters call "udderly delicious" chocolate chip drop cookies in regular cow chip, mini chiplet, and giant bullchip sizes.

Express Cookies

Almost every local cookie store with a website also sells their cookies online, but only a few specialize in it. Here, I check out the chocolate chip offerings from a few of the bigger mail-order cookie companies. (I value my life too much to order homemade chocolate chip cookies through Etsy and eBay, as is now possible.)

Carol's, www.carolscookies.com, $35.50 for 12 cookies plus S/H. (Single cookies also sold for $2 each at many Whole Foods). Carol's cookies get the prize for looks—the elegant brown tins and lumpy-bumpy, 7.2-ounce behemoths are both highly impressive. Sugar is the dominant taste and texture: The cookie is crunchy and crystallized on the outside and like uncooked dough in the center. You will score points for classiness for sending these to your favorite sugar addict. (See Carol's story, opposite page.)

Carol Goldman of Carol's Cookies

Cheryl's, www.cheryls.com, $28.95 per dozen plus S/H. Like David's and Tom's Mom's (see below), this company dates back to the 1980s' retail cookie craze—and, as with the other two companies, its founder (Cheryl Krueger) has long since moved on. The cookies are supermarket-cookie-sized and individually wrapped in plastic with a Nutrition Facts panel, like Mrs. Fields cookies sold in convenience stores, and packed in the kind of cardboard box used by Amazon when they send me books (although Cheryl's website does appear to offer more attractive container options). The overall impression and the taste is of a factory-made cookie. The caramel pecan chocolate chip variation is more worth its 200 calories than the plain. But their buttercream-frosted sugar cookies are terrific and probably the way to go if you're ordering from Cheryl's.

David's, www.davidscookies.com, $24.95 per 1-pound tin (about 12 cookies) plus S/H. Though no longer made by David Liederman, these cookies are soft and flat and contain chocolate chunks, rather than chips, like the old David's. They're also an attractive tan color, a satisfying 3 to 3½ inches in diameter, taste freshly baked and come nicely packaged in a red tin adorned with the David's logo. In short, these are much better than you might expect from a company as big as David's now is.

Tom's Mom's, www.tomsmomscookies.com, $35 for two dozen (minimum order) plus S/H. This business is probably the biggest thing in Harbor Springs, a Michigan town of 1,200 less than 75 miles from the Canadian border. Tom's Mom's manager Sheryl McCleery bought the place from former owner/boss Tom Kneeland in the mid-'90s and has been fielding questions about Tom's mom ever since. Business grew exponentially after Rachael Ray featured Tom's Mom's cinnamon sugar cookies on her show in 2003. In size, their chocolate chunk cookies are somewhere between Carol's and David's. The texture is crumbly and dry and almost healthy tasting: Could it be the winter wheat on the ingredient list? Nuts are big and more prominent than the chocolate. They come stacked 12 to a vertical, liquor bottle–like box decorated with quaint cartoon drawings of a happy-looking family (headed by Tom's mom, presumably).

One of the Lucky People Who Needed "People"

Carol Goldman of suburban Chicago, might still be just another one of thousands of hobby bakers who sell cookies to a few local stores and restaurants, had *People* magazine not called the week of Thanksgiving in 1983.

Tipped off by an admiring local chocolate supplier, the magazine asked Goldman to be part of a national taste test to find the country's best chocolate chip cookie: Could she send three tins of cookies to New York in a few days?

"At first I thought it was one of my girlfriends being funny. At that point I was still baking the cookies out of my house and I had 30 people coming for Thanksgiving dinner," Goldman recalled. Let's just say it wasn't the greatest Thanksgiving meal Carol ever served, as she worked frantically to produce the perfect batch of cookies and find some professional-looking tins to pack them in.

The second crisis came with the second call from *People*, saying she was a finalist and they needed to take her picture. "I spent a week trying to come up with a good outfit" that only the photographer saw: The picture they used gave a whole new, sweeter meaning to the phrase "ring around the collar," featuring, as it did, her head sticking through a box filled with her chocolate chip cookies.

Carol's cookies ended up placing fourth of the seven final entries in the *People* contest feature and were also voted best-looking. Within weeks, Chicago-area newspapers ran their own stories, and, almost overnight, her business tripled. Carol's Cookies was well on its way to being the national mail order cookie company it is today.

Chocolate Chip Cookies: A (Very Short) World Tour

The United States may have lost some of its global economic and political clout, but it remains the world leader in chocolate chip cookies: The cookies and the chips to make them are both pretty hard to find abroad.

Suburban Cleveland, Ohio-based Nestlé® Toll House® marketing director Jim Coyne says he regularly has to send care packages of morsels to friends in England and Switzerland (the latter, presumably colleagues at Nestlé's Swiss world headquarters who might be in a position to bring morsels to that country—so let's get with it, guys!).

American chocolate chip cookies—dubbed "le cookie"—became all the rage in French pastry shops a few years ago, says Paris-based pastry chef, author, and blogger David Lebovitz. The profusion of wonderful bakeries in France means very little baking of chocolate chip cookies or anything else in home kitchens there, Lebovitz adds.

Ziad Dalal, CEO of the Nestlé Toll House Café by Chip chain of dessert cafés, admits that he "had butterflies" upon opening his first international branch in Beirut in 2010, where the term Toll House was unknown and chocolate chip cookies were mainly available at American-based hotels and restaurants, like Starbucks. But positioned as an upscale dessert, served on a plate with silverware and a chocolate sauce garnish, the chocolate chip cookie has become a "huge" international seller, and his Middle East Café by Chip stores are some of the most profitable in his entire 120-store chain.

Mrs. Fields and David's both opened shops in Japan (a few David's continue to operate there today) but their success rested more on the cookie's novelty and American cachet: Chocolate chips are still not integrated into the Japanese culture or widely available there.

Mrs. Fields did less well in England. David's stayed away. "The English are not sophisticated enough about what they eat," he once explained, and if you've ever tried some of the dry biscuits that pass for cookies there, you know what he means.

Otis Spunkmeyer flopped in the U.K., but for a different reason: their name. "Spunk," in Britain and elsewhere, is slang for semen, U.S.-based company executives discovered to their great embarrassment.

Debbi Fields in Japan

5

DIY Chocolate Chip

At least half a dozen previously published cookbooks have purportedly been devoted to the chocolate chip cookie. I say "purportedly" because at least half the recipes in them are for chocolate cookies or peanut butter cookies or any food that has chocolate chips in it. This book has more integrity. Designed for people who love chocolate chip cookies, this recipe chapter maintains a laser-like focus on recipes that deliver the Toll House® taste. You'll also find advice on ingredients and information to help you make exactly the kind of cookie *you* like. This is not to say I won't give you some ideas for spicing up your cookies (in a few cases, quite literally). But in most cases, the primary taste will be of brown sugar, butter, and chocolate, as is only right in a book for chocolate chip cookie lovers.

From a 1954 Nestlé® recipe booklet

Original Nestlé® Toll House® Chocolate Chip Cookies

We are going to start where we should, with the modernized, Nestlé Kitchens–tested version of the recipe that started it all. (See page 24 for the historic recipe.)

2¼ cups all-purpose flour
1 teaspoon baking soda
1 teaspoon salt
1 cup (2 sticks) butter, softened
¾ cup granulated sugar
¾ cup packed brown sugar
1 teaspoon vanilla extract
2 large eggs
2 cups (12 ounces) Nestlé Toll House Semi-Sweet Morsels
1 cup chopped nuts

Original Nestlé Toll House Cookies

Preheat the oven to 375 degrees. Combine the flour, baking soda, and salt in small bowl. Using an electric mixer, beat the butter, granulated sugar, brown sugar, and vanilla in a large bowl until creamy. Add the eggs, one at a time, beating well after each addition. Gradually beat in the flour mixture. Stir in the morsels and nuts. Drop by rounded tablespoonfuls onto ungreased baking sheets. Bake for 9 to 11 minutes or until golden brown. Let cool on the baking sheets for 2 minutes; remove to wire racks to cool completely.

Yield: 60 cookies

Martha's Daughter's Famous Chocolate Chip Cookies

This recipe was inspired by one Alexis Stewart came up with as a 13-year-old on a challenge from her mother Martha, then mainly known as a Connecticut caterer. An employee made a chocolate chip cookie Martha loved, but the worker wouldn't share with the boss lady. "It took me two tries to figure it out," the grown-up Alexis wrote in her 2011 book *Whateverland*. Alexis's cookies bake up flat, crispy and chewy, and big on brown sugar—but skimpy on chocolate. This adaptation fixes that flaw.

1¾ cups all-purpose flour
1 teaspoon baking soda
1 teaspoon salt
1 cup (2 sticks) butter, softened
¾ cup granulated sugar
1¼ cups packed brown sugar
1 teaspoon vanilla extract
2 large eggs
1½ cups (9 ounces) semisweet chocolate chips

Preheat the oven to 375 degrees. Grease two baking sheets lightly. (Do not use parchment paper.) Combine the flour, baking soda, and salt in small bowl. Using an electric mixer, beat the butter, granulated sugar, brown sugar and vanilla extract in a large bowl until creamy. Add the eggs one at a time, beating well after each addition. Gradually beat in the flour mixture. Stir in the chocolate chips and nuts. Form the dough into 1½-inch balls and place on the baking sheets. Bake for 8 to 10 minutes or until golden brown. Cool on the baking sheets for 2 minutes; remove to wire racks to cool completely.

Yield: 40 large cookies.

Cashew Chocolate Chip Crisps

"The best chocolate chip cookies I ever tasted," Ed Levine of *Serious Eats* once said of this chocolate chip cookie riff, a signature offering of James Beard award–winning pastry chef Claudia Fleming at New York's Gramercy Tavern in the late 1990s. Sadly, they are no longer served at Gramercy or at Fleming's current restaurant, North Fork Table and Inn on Long Island. The force of expectation for finding walnuts and semisweet chocolate in a chocolate chip cookie is so strong that the cashews and "milk chocolate chips seemed to be a disappointment for most folks, but I loved them!" says Fleming. The recipe is from Fleming's *Last Course* cookbook.

2½ cups cashews, toasted
2½ cups all-purpose flour
1 teaspoon salt
1 cup unsalted butter, softened
1¼ cups packed light brown sugar
1¼ cups granulated sugar
1 teaspoon vanilla extract
Grated zest from 1 orange
2 large eggs
1¾ teaspoons baking soda
1 teaspoon water
8 ounces bittersweet chocolate, coarsely chopped
8 ounces milk chocolate, coarsely chopped

Preheat the oven to 325 degrees. Line two baking sheets with parchment paper or silicone mats and set aside.

In a food processor, pulse ½ cup of the toasted cashews with 1 tablespoon of the flour to a fine meal. In a medium bowl, combine the remaining flour, salt, and the ground cashew mixture. Coarsely chop the remaining cashews and set aside.

In the bowl of a stand mixer fitted with the paddle attachment, beat the butter, brown sugar, and granulated sugar until creamy and light, about 3 minutes. Add the vanilla and orange zest and mix until well combined. Add the eggs one at a time, beating for a minute after each addition. Dissolve the baking soda in the water and add to the bowl, beating to combine. In two batches, add the flour mixture, blending until just combined. Stir in the chopped chocolate and cashews.

Drop heaping tablespoons of dough onto the prepared baking sheets. Bake for about 18 minutes, rotating the sheets at the halfway point, until the cookies are golden all over. Let cool on racks.

Yield: 36 cookies.

Sour Cream Chocolate Chip Cookies

Sour cream adds not only a touch of tangy richness to these cookies but also moisture that makes them more like mini chocolate chip cakes.

2 cups all-purpose flour
1 teaspoon baking soda
1 teaspoon salt
1 cup (2 sticks) unsalted butter, softened
1 cup granulated sugar
½ cup firmly packed dark brown sugar
2 teaspoons vanilla extract
2 large eggs
½ cup sour cream
1 cup coarsely chopped walnuts (toasted if you have time)
2 cups (12 ounces) semisweet or bittersweet chocolate chips or 12 ounces bar chocolate chopped into ¼-inch pieces

Position two oven racks near the middle of the oven and preheat the oven to 375 degrees. Sift together the flour, baking soda, and salt into a bowl and set aside. In a large mixing bowl, combine the butter, granulated sugar, brown sugar, eggs, and vanilla and beat until creamy. Stir in the sour cream and blend. Add the dry ingredients and blend well. Add the nuts and chocolate chips.

Drop by teaspoonfuls onto ungreased baking sheets, spacing the cookies about 2 inches apart. Bake two sheets at a time, rotating them halfway through the baking time of 10 to 15 minutes until all the cookies are evenly golden brown. After 3 minutes, transfer the cookies to wire racks to finish cooling.

Yield: 48 cookies.

Italian Chocolate Chip Cookies

Another country heard from on the subject of the chocolate chip cookie. Like many Italian cookies, these are biscuit-like.

4 cups all-purpose flour
1 teaspoon baking powder
¼ teaspoon salt
½ cup water
½ cup olive oil
½ cup packed light brown sugar
1 cup (6 ounces) semisweet chocolate chips
¼ cup pine nuts
Confectioners' sugar

Preheat the oven to 375 degrees. Sift together the flour, baking powder, and salt and set aside. In a large bowl, combine the water, oil, and sugar. Gradually add the flour mixture until well combined. Add the chocolate chips and pine nuts. Drop 2-teaspoon-sized portions onto ungreased baking sheets. Bake for 12 minutes. Let cool and then sprinkle with confectioners' sugar. Store in airtight containers.

Yield: 78 cookies

Pudding Chocolate Chip Cookies

A convenience-product-recipe favorite of fans of soft and cakelike chocolate chip cookies.

1 cup (2 sticks) butter or margarine, softened

¾ cup packed brown sugar

¼ cup granulated sugar

1 (3.4-ounce) box instant vanilla pudding

1 teaspoon vanilla extract

2 large eggs

1 teaspoon baking soda

2¼ cups flour

2 cups (12 ounces) semisweet chocolate chips

1 cup chopped nuts (optional)

Pudding Chocolate Chip Cookies

Preheat the oven to 375 degrees. Combine butter, brown sugar, granulated sugar, pudding mix, and vanilla in a large bowl and stir until well blended. Add eggs; mix well. Add baking soda and then gradually add flour. Stir in chocolate chips and nuts, if using.

Drop teaspoonfuls of dough 2 inches apart onto ungreased baking sheets. Bake 8 to 10 minutes or until golden brown. Let cool 3 minutes then transfer to wire racks to cool completely.

Yield: about 60 cookies

Passover Chocolate Chip Cookies

The Passover meal is meant to symbolically recall the dinner ancient Jews grabbed before escaping Pharaoh's clutches, and so no foods leavened with yeast or baked with traditional flour are allowed. Jews have struggled to come up with a decent Passover chocolate chip cookie ever since. Most attempts substitute with matzo (unleavened) bread flour, potato starch, and ground nuts or some combination (as here). If your cookies must also be parve, you'll need to use vegetable shortening or pesach margarine instead of butter, and parve chocolate chips.

1 cup (2 sticks) butter, room temperature
1½ cups packed brown sugar
2 large eggs
1 tablespoon vanilla extract
1 cup matzo cake meal
¼ cup matzo meal
½ cup potato starch
1½ teaspoons baking soda (kosher for Passover)
2 cups (12 ounces) semisweet chocolate chips
1 cup chopped nuts (optional)

Preheat the oven to 350 degrees. Generously grease two baking sheets. In a large bowl, cream the butter and sugar. Add the eggs and vanilla and mix well. Gradually blend in the matzo cake meal, matzo meal, potato starch, and soda. Mix in the chocolate chips and nuts, if using. Drop the batter by rounded tablespoonfuls onto the baking sheets, leaving 1 inch between. Bake for 6 to 8 minutes, or until light brown.

Yield: 48 cookies

Vegan Chocolate Chip Cookies

No animal products allowed: That's the basic deal with vegans. Bakers approach this many different ways, depending on whether veganism is their only concern (vegans being often also interested in using natural ingredients and eating healthy). The below recipe limits the barriers to good taste just to the traditional chocolate chip cookie's animal-derived egg, butter, and (possibly) chocolate chips. As with most vegan recipes, this one could also work for people with dairy allergies.

2¼ cups all-purpose flour
1 teaspoon baking soda
1 teaspoon salt
1 cup nondairy margarine (such as Earth Balance)
1 cup packed light brown sugar
½ cup granulated sugar
1 teaspoon vanilla extract
1–3 tablespoons water
2 cups (12 ounces) dairy-free semisweet chocolate chips (like Tropical Source)

Preheat the oven to 350 degrees. Combine the flour, baking soda, and salt in a small bowl. Using an electric mixer, beat the margarine, brown sugar, granulated sugar, and vanilla in a large bowl until fluffy. Add 1 tablespoon of the water. Gradually beat in the flour mixture, adding additional water if necessary to attain the proper dough consistency. Stir in the chocolate chips. Drop by rounded tablespoonfuls onto ungreased baking sheets. Bake for 8 to 10 minutes or until light brown. Let cool on the baking sheets for 2 minutes; transfer to wire racks to cool completely.

Yield: 36 cookies

Diet Chocolate Chip Cookies

The best diet chocolate chip cookies are smaller versions of really good ones or really good ones eaten less frequently. But since this is a recipe chapter, here is a reduced-fat and -calorie recipe. I'll let you decide whether or not to beef it up with whole-wheat flour or bran (to help fill you up; see page 170 for how to do this) or replace the sugar with a low-calorie sugar substitute (according to the manufacturer's instructions).

6 tablespoons packed brown sugar
6 tablespoons granulated sugar
¼ cup applesauce
2 tablespoons vegetable shortening
1 large egg white
½ teaspoon vanilla extract
1 cup all-purpose flour
½ teaspoon baking soda
½ teaspoon salt
¾ cup semisweet chocolate chips (or less, to cut even more calories)

Preheat the oven to 375 degrees. Lightly grease two baking sheets. In a medium bowl, combine the brown sugar, granulated sugar, applesauce, and shortening. Add the egg white and vanilla and mix thoroughly. In a separate bowl, combine the flour, baking soda, and salt. Gradually blend the flour mixture into the wet ingredients. Mix in the chocolate chips. Drop by well-rounded teaspoonfuls onto baking sheets. Bake 8 to 12 minutes or until lightly browned. Let cool on the baking sheets for 3 minutes, then transfer to wire racks to cool completely.

Yield: about 24 cookies

Gluten-Free Flour Blend for Chocolate Chip Cookies

Suddenly, it seems, there's an epidemic of people in this country with an allergy to gluten, present in wheat, barley, and rye flours, and who therefore can't eat traditional chocolate chip cookies. (Pause here to join me in a moment of deep sympathy.) Celiac sufferers can only eat chocolate chip cookies that have been made with substitute flour blends like the following. This blend can be swapped in, cup for cup, for regular all-purpose flour in almost any chocolate chip cookie recipe, although the taste will be different, and the texture somewhat gritty.

1¼ cups white rice flour
1 cup brown rice flour
¾ cup sweet rice flour
⅔ cup tapioca starch flour
¼ cup potato starch flour
⅓ cup cornstarch
2 teaspoons xanthan or guar gum

Combine all the ingredients and mix thoroughly. Use immediately or store in an airtight container in the refrigerator or freezer. (The mix will keep up to 8 months if refrigerated and up to 1 year if frozen.)

Yield: 4½ cups mix

Chocolate Chip Pizza (aka Giant Cookie)

An alternative to bankruptcy for Mrs. Fields fanatics: Instructions for making a cookie that should keep you in the chips for at least a week.

1 cup all-purpose flour
⅛ teaspoon baking soda
½ teaspoon salt
⅓ cup butter or margarine, softened
½ cup firmly packed brown sugar
½ cup granulated sugar
1 large egg
1 teaspoon vanilla extract
1 cup (6 ounces) semisweet chocolate chips
½ cup chopped nuts

Adjust an oven rack to the middle position and preheat the oven to 350 degrees. Combine the flour, baking soda, and salt and set aside. In a large bowl, beat the butter with the brown sugar and granulated sugar. Add the egg and vanilla. Mix in the flour mixture, one-third at a time. Add the chocolate chips and nuts. Turn the dough out onto an ungreased baking sheet or pizza pan and, with floured hands, pat and shape it into a 10-inch-diameter disk. Bake for 15 minutes or until the edges and top are light golden brown. Let cool about 7 minutes, then run a large spatula under the cookie to release it from the pan. Leave in the pan to complete cooling.

Yield: 12 to 15 servings

Chocolate Chip Freezer Cookies

Be prepared for any cookie emergency by having this artificial-ingredient-free chocolate chip cookie dough in your freezer. Substituting vegetable oil for some of the butter makes the frozen logs easier to slice—it's an idea I borrowed from Nancy Baggett's excellent *All-American Cookie Book.*

1½ cups all-purpose flour

1½ teaspoons baking powder

½ teaspoon salt

½ cup (1 stick) butter, room temperature

¼ cup canola or other flavorless vegetable oil

½ cup packed brown sugar

½ cup granulated sugar

1 large egg

1 teaspoon vanilla extract

1 cup (6 ounces) mini semisweet chocolate chips

Mix the flour, baking powder, and salt together in a small bowl. In a large bowl, beat together the butter, vegetable oil, brown sugar, and granulated sugar. Add the egg and vanilla and beat until light and fluffy. Add the dry ingredients, mixing well. Stir in the chocolate chips. Divide the dough in half and shape each piece into a log about 2 inches wide and 7 inches long. (You can also make more smaller logs or individual dough balls, depending on the size of your family and your chocolate chip cookie–eating habits.) Wrap the logs tightly in plastic wrap (or place the balls in a pan) and refrigerate until firm, about 1 hour. Then place the logs (or balls) in a tightly closed plastic bag and freeze for up to 2 months.

To bake, preheat the oven to 350 degrees. Take the logs out of the freezer and let sit at room temperature before unwrapping. Slice into ¼-inch-thick slices for crisp cookies; up to 1-inch-thick slices for larger, softer ones. Place slices 2 inches apart on ungreased baking sheet and bake for 10 to 12 minutes or until golden around the edges. Gently transfer to wire rack to cool.

Yield: 36 cookies

Make-Ahead Chocolate Chip Cookie Mix

Here's another do-ahead chocolate chip cookie recipe that won't use up freezer space. But you must like the Toll House® recipe (on which this is based) made with shelf-stable shortening instead of perishable butter. Credit for the idea belongs to Marian Burros, who created a sensation when she wrote about this in the *New York Times* in 1985.

9 cups all-purpose flour
3 cups firmly packed brown sugar
3 cups granulated sugar
4 teaspoons baking soda
2 teaspoons salt
4 cups vegetable shortening
8 cups (48 ounces) semisweet chocolate chips
4 cups chopped nuts (optional)

In a very large bowl, combine the flour, brown sugar, granulated sugar, baking soda, and salt. Thoroughly blend the shortening in with your fingers. Stir in the chocolate chips and nuts, if using. Store in an airtight container in cool, dry place for up to 6 months; up to a year if frozen.

Yield: about 28 cups mix

When ready to make: Preheat the oven to 375 degrees. Grease some baking sheets. Put 7 cups of the mix (or 6 if you're not using nuts) into a large bowl and stir to distribute mix-ins evenly. Add 2 slightly beaten eggs and 1 1/2 teaspoons vanilla. The batter will be somewhat stiff. Drop heaping tablespoonfuls of batter onto the baking sheets and bake for 10 to 12 minutes.

Yield: 2 dozen cookies

Cake Mix Chocolate Chip Cookies

Yellow cake mix supplies the sugar and flour in this time-honored chocolate chip convenience recipe. It produces a soft, quite sweet, and, not surprisingly, cakelike chocolate chip cookie with a yellow hue that could set lemon lovers up for disappointment.

1 (16.5-ounce) package yellow cake mix

½ cup (1 stick) butter, softened

2 large eggs

2 tablespoons milk

1 teaspoon vanilla extract

2 cups (12 ounces) semisweet chocolate chips

Preheat the oven to 350 degrees. Pour the cake mix into a large bowl. Stir in the butter, eggs, milk, and vanilla until well blended. Stir in the chocolate chips. Drop by rounded teaspoonfuls onto baking sheets. Bake for 11 to 15 minutes, until the edges are golden. Let cool on the baking sheets for a few minutes before removing to cool on wire racks.

Yield: 48 cookies

Chocolate Chip Madeleines

A recipe has got to be unusual and not stray too far from the Toll House® taste to earn a place in this chapter. This 2001 Nestlé® contest winner meets both criteria while bridging Franco-American cookie culture. It combines the French favorite, shell-shaped madeleines, with the all-American chocolate chip, just the way recipe creator Ronda Smith did in her own family when she married a Frenchman.

4 large eggs
1 cup granulated sugar
1 teaspoon vanilla extract
1 tablespoon Cointreau (optional)
Grated zest from 1 orange
2 cups all-purpose flour
1⅓ cups Nestlé Toll House Semi-Sweet Chocolate Morsels, divided
1 cup (2 sticks) unsalted butter, melted
Confectioners' sugar

Preheat the oven to 350 degrees. Grease and flour a madeleine pan. Combine the eggs, sugar, vanilla, Cointreau, if using, and orange zest in the bowl of a stand mixer fitted with the whisk attachment. Beat the mixture until light in color. In a separate bowl, mix the flour and 1 cup of the morsels. Fold the flour mixture and butter alternately into the egg mixture, beginning and ending with the flour. Pour into the prepared pan. Bake for 10 to 12 minutes or until golden around edges. Let cool, then sprinkle with confectioners' sugar. Cool, clean and re-flour and re-grease the pan twice to make the other two dozen cookies. Microwave the remaining ⅓ cup morsels in a small bowl. Drizzle over the madeleines.

Yield: 36 cookies

Chocolate Chip Cookie Pancakes

Chocolate chip pancakes are great but a tad too subtle compared to pancakes containing actual pieces of chocolate chip cookie.

8 crisp 2-inch chocolate chip cookies (store-bought or homemade)
1 cup all-purpose flour
3 tablespoons brown sugar
1¾ teaspoons baking powder
1 teaspoon salt
1 cup milk, plus extra if needed
1 large egg
1 teaspoon vanilla extract
2 tablespoons butter, melted
½ cup mini semisweet chocolate chips

Place the cookies in a plastic bag and crush with a rolling pin into ½-inch pieces. In a large bowl, sift together the flour, sugar, baking powder, and salt. In a separate bowl, whisk together the milk, egg, and vanilla; add to the flour mixture, stirring only until smooth. Blend in the melted butter and cookie crumbs. If the batter seems too thick to pour, add a little more milk. Pour about ¼ cup of batter on a hot, greased griddle for each pancake, immediately sprinkling 1½ teaspoons of mini chocolate chips onto each. Cook the pancakes until bubbly, a little dry around the edges, and lightly browned on the bottom; turn and brown the other side. Serve.

Yield: 8 to 10 pancakes.

Toll House® Sour Cream Crumb Cake

Chocolate chip cookies for breakfast? Not quite, but this crumb cake does offer some of the same tastes.

Topping

⅓ cup packed brown sugar

1 tablespoon all-purpose flour

2 tablespoons butter or margarine, softened

½ cup chopped nuts

½ cup Nestlé® Toll House Semi-Sweet Chocolate Mini Morsels

Cake

1¾ cups all-purpose flour

1 teaspoon baking powder

1 teaspoon baking soda

¼ teaspoon salt

¾ cup granulated sugar

½ cup (1 stick) butter or margarine, softened

1 teaspoon vanilla extract

3 large eggs

1 cup sour cream

1½ cups (9 ounces) Nestlé Toll House Semi-Sweet Chocolate Mini Morsels

Preheat the oven to 350 degrees. Grease a 13 x 9-inch baking pan.

For the topping: Combine the brown sugar, flour, and butter in a small bowl with a pastry blender or two knives until the mixture is crumbly. Stir in the nuts and mini morsels and set aside.

For the cake: Combine the flour, baking powder, baking soda, and salt in a small bowl. Using an electric mixer, beat the butter, sugar, and vanilla in a large bowl until creamy. Add the eggs, one at a time, beating well after each addition. Gradually add the flour mixture alternately with the sour cream. Fold in the mini morsels. Spread into the prepared pan; sprinkle with the topping. Bake 25 to 35 minutes or until a wooden pick inserted in the center comes out clean. Let cool in the pan on a wire rack.

Yield: 12 servings

Toll House Sour Cream Crumb Cake

Chocolate Chip Nut Cheese Ball

This is a chocolate chip cookie lover's sweet variation on the classic 1970s party appetizer.

1 (8-ounce) package cream cheese, softened
½ cup butter, softened
¾ cup confectioners' sugar
2 tablespoons brown sugar
¼ teaspoon vanilla extract
¾ cup mini semisweet chocolate chips
¾ cup walnuts (or other nut), finely chopped
Graham crackers

In a medium bowl, beat together the cream cheese and butter until fluffy. Mix in the confectioners' sugar, brown sugar, and vanilla. Stir in the chocolate chips. Cover and refrigerate for 2 hours. Shape the chilled cream cheese mixture into a ball. Wrap with plastic; return to the refrigerator for at least another 2 hours. Roll the cheese ball in nuts and let sit at room temperature for 30 minutes before serving with graham crackers.

Yield: 8 to 12 servings

Chocolate Chip Nut Cheese Ball

Chocolate Chip Cookie Milk Shake

A recipe tailor-made for cookie dunkers.

3 cups vanilla ice cream

1 cup milk

¼ cup mini semisweet chocolate chips

4 hard supermarket chocolate chip cookies (such as Chips Ahoy or Chips Deluxe)

Whipped cream, for topping (optional)

Put all the ingredients in a blender or food processor with a metal blade and blend until frothy. Pour into glasses and top with whipped cream, if desired.

Yield: 2 to 3 shakes

Chocolate Chip Cheesecake

Chocolate chip cookies in cheesecake form.

18 hard packaged chocolate chip cookies, finely crushed (about 1½ cups)
¼ cup (½ stick) salted butter or margarine, melted
2 (8-ounce) packages cream cheese, softened
¾ cup packed light brown sugar
¼ cup granulated sugar
2 cups sour cream
3 large eggs
2 cups (12 ounces) dark or semisweet chocolate chips or chunks

Chocolate Chip Cheesecake

Preheat the oven to 350 degrees. Blend the crumbs and butter in a small bowl and then press onto the bottom of a 9-inch springform pan. Place in the refrigerator.

Beat the cream cheese, brown sugar, and granulated sugar in a large bowl until blended. Add the sour cream; mix well. Add the eggs, one at a time, beating until blended. Stir about three-quarters of the chocolate chips into the batter. Pour the batter into the crust. Sprinkle the remaining chocolate evenly over the top.

Place the springform pan in the oven (above a pizza pan or baking sheet to catch drips) and bake 35 to 45 minutes or until the center is almost set. Turn the oven off and leave the cheesecake in the oven for 1 hour to set. Run a knife around the rim of the pan to loosen the cake. Refrigerate for at least 3 hours. Remove the rim of the pan and serve.

Yield: 12 servings.

Toll House® Pie (aka Chocolate Chip Pie)

This is similar to a Southern pecan, Pennsylvania Dutch shoofly, or Kentucky Derby pie. Never had them? Then think chocolate chip cookie baked in a pie crust. This recipe is courtesy of Toll House morsel–maker Nestlé®. You can use a homemade or store-bought crust; if frozen, allow it to thaw before using.

2 large eggs
½ cup all-purpose flour
½ cup granulated sugar
½ cup packed brown sugar
¾ cup (1½ sticks) butter, softened
1 cup (6 ounces) Nestlé Toll House Semi-Sweet Chocolate Morsels
1 cup chopped walnuts or pecans
1 9-inch (4-cup volume) deep-dish pie shell, unbaked
Sweetened whipped cream (optional)

Preheat the oven to 325 degrees. Using an electric mixer, beat the eggs in a large bowl on high speed until foamy. Beat in the flour, granulated sugar, and brown sugar. Beat in the butter, then stir in the morsels and nuts. Spoon the mixture into the pie shell. Bake for 55 to 60 minutes or until a knife inserted halfway between the edge and center comes out clean. Let cool on a wire rack. Serve warm with whipped cream, if desired.

Yield: 10 servings

Tate's Refrigerator Cake

This is a chocolate chip cookie adaptation of the famous (and famously easy) back-of-the-box recipe using Nabisco Famous Chocolate Wafers. It will only work with very thin chocolate chip cookies like Tate's. Don't use cookies containing nuts, since they'll get soggy.

2 cups heavy cream

1 teaspoon vanilla extract

12–15 Tate's (or other very thin) chocolate chip cookies without nuts

Mini chocolate chips

Using an electric mixer, beat the cream on high speed until stiff peaks form. Gently stir in the vanilla. Spread 1½ teaspoons of whipped cream on each cookie; stack the cookies together, then stand the stack on its side on a platter. Frost with the remaining whipped cream. Sprinkle with mini chocolate chips. Refrigerate for 4 hours. Cut into diagonal slices to serve.

Yield: 10 to 12 servings

Chocolate Chip Whoopie Pies

The classic whoopie pie is a vanilla crème-filled chocolate cake sandwich originating in Pennsylvania Amish country and/or Maine (there is debate) in the 1920s. This chocolate chip version is among the more tame whoopie flavor variations available since the whoopie became all the rage at upscale bake shops. (It's much better than lemon lavender, believe me.)

Cookies

2½ cups all-purpose flour
½ teaspoon baking soda
½ teaspoon salt
½ cup (1 stick) butter, softened
½ cup packed brown sugar
1 cup milk
1 large egg
1 teaspoon vanilla extract
1 cup (6 ounces) semisweet chocolate chips

Filling

1⅓ cups marshmallow crème
1 cup vegetable shortening
1 cup confectioners' sugar
¼ teaspoon salt
1 tablespoon water
1½ teaspoons vanilla extract
1 cup (6 ounces) mini semisweet chocolate chips (optional)

For the cookies: Preheat the oven to 350 degrees. Line two baking sheets with parchment paper or lightly grease them. Combine the flour, baking soda, and salt in small bowl. Using an electric mixer, beat the butter and sugar in a large bowl on medium speed until light and fluffy. Beat in the milk, egg, and vanilla (the mixture will be thin). Beat in the flour mixture on low speed until smooth. Stir in the chocolate chips. Drop by ¼-cupfuls onto the prepared baking sheets, leaving plenty of room between the cakes. (You should have 16 cookies.) Bake for 15 to 16 minutes until springy to the touch. Let cool completely on the baking sheets.

For the filling: Beat the marshmallow crème, shortening, and sugar with an electric mixer until well combined. Dissolve the salt in the water and add to the marshmallow mixture. Add the vanilla and beat. Spread the filling on the flat side one of the cooled cookies and top with the flat side of another cookie to make a sandwich. Repeat with the other cookies. Spread the chocolate chips on a plate and roll the edges of all the whoopie pies in them, if desired. If not eating immediately, wrap the sandwiches individually in plastic.

Yield: 8 large whoopie pies

Chocolate Chip Cookie Pudding

This is a chocolate chip–spiked pudding with a mild brown sugar flavor. Lazy people who make their chocolate chip cookies with dark brown sugar might be just as happy sprinkling some mini chocolate chips on Jell-O Instant Butterscotch Pudding.

¼ cup (½ stick) butter
1 cup packed light brown sugar
½ teaspoon salt
2 cups whole milk
½ cup heavy cream
3 tablespoons cornstarch
2 large eggs
1 teaspoon vanilla extract
½ cup mini semisweet chocolate chips

Chocolate Chip Cookie Pudding

Melt the butter in a medium-sized saucepan over medium heat. Turn the heat up to medium-high, add the sugar and salt, then stir until the sugar and butter blend and bubble up. Add 1¾ cups of the milk and the cream and remove from the heat.

In a small bowl, beat the remaining ¼ milk with the cornstarch and beat in the eggs. Pour this mixture into the pan with the sugar-butter mixture and return to medium heat. Cook, stirring constantly, until thickened. Remove from the heat and stir in vanilla. Pour into a 2-quart casserole dish or individual serving glasses and chill thoroughly, at least 4 hours. Top with the chocolate chips before serving.

Yield: 4 to 6 servings

Toll House® Trifle

A highly Americanized version of a traditional English dessert. For a milder flavor, use vanilla pudding.

¾ cup cold milk
1 (3.5-ounce) package butterscotch or vanilla instant pudding
1 (8-ounce) tub Cool Whip, thawed, or 1½ cups heavy cream, whipped
27 (2-inch) packaged chocolate chip cookies (such as Chips Ahoy or Chips Deluxe)

Combine the milk and pudding mix in a large bowl and whisk for 2 minutes. Stir in the Cool Whip. Arrange 9 cookies on the bottom of an 8-inch square casserole or baking dish; top with one-third of the pudding mixture. Repeat layering two more times; cover. Refrigerate for several hours or overnight before serving.

Yield: 6 servings

Mailing and Storage

Sharing your cookies with someone far away? Thick and sturdy chocolate chip cookies obviously will stand up to Postal Service or express mail transport much better than the thin and crumbly kinds. Put two cookies back to back and wrap the duo loosely in aluminum foil or waxed paper and pack them in non-overlapping layers in a small sturdy box (like a shoe box), filling in any empty space with bubble wrap or Styrofoam peanuts.

Saving your cookies for another day? Fresh-baked cookies will stay that way for about three days. Store soft cookies in an airtight container or bags and crispy ones out in the open if you want them to retain those textures. Freshly made chocolate chip cookies placed in airtight bags can be frozen quite successfully for months.

As for the plastic wrap–mummy treatment given to baked goods, including chocolate chip cookies, at coffee shops that bake infrequently or not at all: It traps moisture and turns even crispy cookies soft. Anyone who likes crisp cookies or freshly baked cookies of any kind should get their baked goods elsewhere.

High Test Toll House® Trifle

Similar to the Toll House Trifle only a bit more indulgent. For those familiar with the pudding and cookies dessert served by Miami's Yellow Submarine food truck, this is an Anglo version. (Theirs uses Goya Maria Mexican butter cookies.)

2 (3.5-ounce) boxes butterscotch or vanilla instant pudding
4 cups cold milk
1 cup heavy cream (unwhipped), plus whipped cream for garnish
1 (14-ounce) can sweetened condensed milk
8 ounces packaged (2-inch) chocolate chip cookies, such as Chips Ahoy, plus extra for garnish

Make the pudding with the milk according to package directions. Let sit 5 minutes. Then add the heavy cream and condensed milk, mixing well. Spread a thin layer of the pudding mixture in the bottom of a 12-inch-diameter, round (preferably glass) bowl. Add a layer of cookies, then another layer of pudding and repeat until all the pudding and cookies are gone. Refrigerate for at least 2 hours, garnish with whipped cream and crushed cookies if desired, then slice and serve.

Yield: 8 to 10 servings

Chocolate Chip Pudding Pie

A chocolate chip variation on a classic Cool Whip dessert.

18 packaged chocolate chip cookies such as Chips Ahoy, finely crushed (about 1½ cups), plus 5 cookies crushed to ¼- to ½-inch pieces

¼ cup (½ stick) butter or margarine, melted

2 (3.5-ounce) packages butterscotch or vanilla instant pudding

2½ cups cold milk

1 (8-ounce) tub Cool Whip, thawed, or 1½ cups heavy cream, whipped

¼ cup mini semisweet chocolate chips

¼ cup chopped walnuts or pecans

Stir together the finely crushed cookies and melted butter and press into a 9-inch pie pan. Combine the pudding mix and milk in a large bowl and whisk for 2 minutes. Stir in half the Cool Whip and the cookie pieces. Pour into the crust. Refrigerate 4 hours or until firm. Top with the remaining Cool Whip, the chocolate chips, and nuts just before serving.

Yield: 10 servings

Chocolate Chip Ice Cream Tartlets

This is a chocolate chip cookie riff on the elegant and easy sugar cookie ice cream cups that won the Pillsbury Bake-Off in 2010.

1 (16.5-ounce) package refrigerated scored chocolate chip cookie dough bar
⅓ cup walnuts, finely chopped
¾ cup mini semisweet chocolate chips
1½ cups chocolate chip ice cream or cookie dough ice cream, softened

Preheat the oven to 325 degrees. Spray 24 mini muffin cups with nonstick cooking spray. Break apart the cookie dough bar and place 1 cookie dough square in each muffin cup. Bake 10 to 12 minutes or until the cookies have spread to the edges of the cups. Press the end of a wooden spoon into each cookie while still warm to make a 1-inch-wide indentation. Let the cookies cool completely in the muffin pans, about 20 minutes.

Meanwhile, place the chopped walnuts in a small bowl. In another small microwavable bowl, microwave ½ cup of the chocolate chips uncovered on high 30 to 60 seconds, stirring after 30 seconds, until smooth.

Run a knife around the edges of the cookies to loosen them; gently remove from the pans. Dip the rim of each cookie "cup" into the melted chocolate, then into the walnuts. Place walnut side up on a rimmed baking sheet. Freeze the cups about 5 minutes or until the chocolate is set.

Spoon the ice cream into the cups, using a small cookie scoop or measuring tablespoon. Top each cup with the rest of the chocolate chips and serve immediately or freeze in a sealed container. If storing, let the tartlets stand at room temperature for 5 minutes before serving.

Yield: 24 tartlets

Chocolate Chip Ice Cream Pie

This recipe is like a larger version of the ice cream tartlets and, like the tartlets, it's the kind of low-work, high-impact dessert that's great for a party. I first encountered a chocolate cookie crust version of this at a Chart House seafood restaurant, where it was rather unappetizingly called mud pie.

18 packaged chocolate chip cookies such as Chips Ahoy, finely crushed (about 1½ cups), plus 5 cookies crushed to ¼- to ½-inch pieces
¼ cup (½ stick) butter or margarine, melted
1 quart chocolate chip or chocolate chip cookie dough or caramel ice cream, softened slightly
1½ cups dark chocolate fudge sauce, store-bought or homemade (see below), placed in the freezer for 15 minutes to aid spreading
Whipped cream (optional)
Mini semisweet chocolate chips, chopped nuts, or more crushed chocolate chip cookies (optional)

Preheat the oven to 350 degrees. Stir together the finely crushed cookies and melted butter and press into a 9-inch pie pan. Bake for 8 to 10 minutes or until the crust is firm around the edges. Let cool completely. Pack the ice cream into the crust and freeze until the ice cream is firm. With a blunt knife, "frost" the ice cream with the thickened chocolate sauce. Place in the freezer uncovered for 20 minutes or until the sauce is set. Then cover tightly with plastic wrap and freeze for 8 to 10 hours. Slice and serve on chilled plates, topped with whipped cream and chocolate chips, nuts, or (to really push the chocolate chip cookie theme) crushed cookies, if desired.

Yield: 8 to 10 slices

Easy Fudge Sauce: Melt 1 cup (6 ounces) semisweet chocolate chips with ¼ cup heavy cream, 1 tablespoon butter, and ½ teaspoon vanilla extract in a saucepan over low heat or in the microwave. Stir until smooth.

Toll House® Layer Cake

I know it's traditional for chocolate chip cookie lovers to celebrate birthdays with a decorated giant cookie (see page 133 for instructions on baking one), but for a change of pace, why not try this layer cake featuring some of the Toll House's traditional walnut, butterscotch and chocolate flavors? Birthday long past? Let your excuse be Ruth Wakefield's birthday (June 17) or Chocolate Chip Cookie Day (May 15).

Cake

2 cups cake flour

3/4 cup packed light brown sugar

3 teaspoons baking powder

1 teaspoon salt

½ cup butter-flavored vegetable shortening

¾ cup milk

¼ cup granulated sugar

2 large eggs

1 teaspoon vanilla extract

2 cups (12 ounces) semisweet chocolate chips, divided

1 cup walnuts, finely chopped, divided

Icing

½ cup (1 stick) butter

1 cup packed light brown sugar

⅓ cup heavy cream

2 cups confectioners' sugar

1 teaspoon vanilla extract

For the cake: Preheat the oven to 350 degrees. Grease and flour two 8-inch round cake pans. Sift the flour, brown sugar, baking powder, and salt into a large bowl. Blend in the shortening, milk, and granulated sugar and beat for 2 minutes. Add the eggs and vanilla. Blend well, then pour into the cake pans. Sprinkle all but about 2 tablespoons of the chocolate chips evenly over the top of the batter in the two pans. Do the same with all but 2 tablespoons of the chopped nuts. Bake for 30 to 40 minutes or until the center of the cakes springs back when lightly touched. Let cool in the pans for 10 minutes, then turn out onto wire racks and let cool completely.

For the icing: Melt the butter in a medium saucepan over medium heat and stir in the brown sugar and cream. Remove from the heat and stir until smooth. Return to medium heat and bring to a boil for 1 minute. Let cool, then beat in the confectioners' sugar and vanilla. Spread the icing on the cooled cake, then decorate with the reserved chocolate chips and nuts.

Yield: 12 to 16 servings

Chocolate Chip, Oats, 'n Caramel Cookie Squares

A Pillsbury Bake-Off–winning layer bar that starts with chocolate chip cookie dough and feeds a crowd.

1 (16.5-ounce) package Pillsbury refrigerated chocolate chip cookie dough
1 cup quick-cooking oats
Pinch salt (optional)
⅔ cup caramel ice cream topping
5 tablespoons Pillsbury Best all-purpose flour
1 teaspoon vanilla extract
¾ cup Fisher chopped walnuts
1 cup Hershey's semi-sweet chocolate chips

Chocolate Chip, Oats, 'n Caramel Cookie Squares

Preheat the oven to 350 degrees. Break up the cookie dough and place in a large bowl. Stir or knead in the oats and salt. Reserve ½ cup of the dough for the topping. Press the remaining dough evenly into an ungreased 9-inch square pan. Bake 10 to 12 minutes or until the dough puffs and appears dry.

Meanwhile, in a small bowl, mix the caramel topping, flour, and vanilla until well blended. Sprinkle the walnuts and chocolate chips evenly over the crust. Drizzle evenly with the caramel mixture. Crumble the reserved ½ cup dough mixture over caramel. Bake 20 to 25 minutes longer or until golden brown. Let cool for 10 minutes. Run a knife around the sides of the pan to loosen the bars. Let cool completely, about 1½ hours. Cut into 4 rows by 4 rows. Store tightly covered.

Yield: 16 bars

Blondies

These are exactly what they sound like: brownies without the cocoa, or chocolate chip cookies in dense bar form. Add a cup of sweetened flaked coconut and they become Congo bars, named for one place coconuts grow.

2¼ cups all-purpose flour

2 teaspoons baking powder

¼ teaspoon salt

¾ cup (1½ sticks) butter

1¾ cups firmly packed brown sugar

3 large eggs

2 teaspoons vanilla extract

1 cup chopped walnuts

1 cup (6 ounces) semisweet chocolate chips

Preheat the oven to 325 degrees. Grease a 9 x 13-inch baking pan. In a medium bowl, combine the flour, baking powder, and salt. In a large bowl, cream the butter and brown sugar until fluffy. Then add the eggs, one at a time, and the vanilla. Add the flour mixture gradually, until well blended. Stir in the nuts and chocolate chips. Spread the batter evenly into the prepared pan. Bake for 35 minutes, or until the top springs back when lightly tapped with a finger. Remove the pan to a wire rack and let cool before cutting.

Yield: 24 bars

Chocolate Chip Cookie-Topped Brownies

A newly popular amalgam of cookie and brownie for those who can't decide between the two. The brownies are based on a recipe from an old Saco Chocolate recipe pamphlet, and are wonderful all on their own should you run out of cooking steam partway through the recipe.

¾ cup (1½ sticks) butter
4 ounces unsweetened baking chocolate
2 cups granulated sugar
4 large eggs
2 teaspoons vanilla extract
1 cup all-purpose flour
½ teaspoon salt
2 cups (12 ounces) semisweet chocolate chips or chunks
1 cup nuts, chopped (optional)
½ recipe Original Nestlé® Toll House Chocolate Chip Cookies (page 123), unbaked, 1½ cups any other chocolate chip cookie dough, or 1 (16.5-ounce) package refrigerated chocolate chip cookie dough

Preheat the oven to 350 degrees. Grease a 9 x 13-inch baking pan, line it with waxed paper or parchment paper, and then grease it again. Heat the butter and chocolate squares in a medium pan until melted and blended. Add the sugar, then the eggs, one at a time. Stir in the vanilla, flour and salt, then add the chocolate chips and nuts, if using, being careful not to overbeat. Spread in the pan. Drop the cookie dough in large spoonfuls onto the brownie batter. Using a spatula, carefully spread the cookie dough evenly over the brownie batter.

Bake 30 to 40 minutes, or until the cookie top is golden brown and a knife inserted into the center of the brownie comes out with only a few moist crumbs attached. When completely cool, run a knife between the pan and the brownies, invert them, remove the paper and turn right side up again.

Yield: 36 brownies
Note: These can also be made in six well-greased 4-inch pie tins, as they are at Baked bakery in Brooklyn (see page 103), or one standard muffin tin, also well-greased, with a shortened bake time (about 20 minutes).

Nestlé® Toll House® Truffles

This is Nestlé's take on a popular (and not coincidentally easy!) candy recipe that could also obviously be made with crushed fresh-baked or store-packaged cookies.

1 (16.5-ounce) package Nestlé Toll House Chocolate Chip Cookie Dough Bar

1 (3-ounce) package cream cheese, room temperature

1 cup (6 ounces) Nestlé Toll House Semi-Sweet Chocolate Morsels

1 tablespoon vegetable shortening

1 tablespoon Nestlé Toll House cocoa or finely crushed walnuts, for dusting (optional)

Preheat the oven to 350 degrees. Prepare the cookies following the package directions; however, bake for 14 to 18 minutes until crisp and golden brown but not burnt. (Crisp cookies are easier to process.) Let the cookies cool completely on wire racks.

Line a baking sheet with waxed paper. Crumble the cookies into a food processor and process until the mixture resembles coarse meal. Add the cream cheese and process until the mixture begins to hold together. (If you have a small food processor, process the cookies and cream cheese in two batches.) Roll or scoop the mixture into 1-inch balls and place on the prepared baking sheet. Refrigerate for 1 hour.

Microwave the morsels and shortening in a small, uncovered, microwave-safe bowl on high power for 1 minute; stir. If necessary, microwave at additional 10- to 15-second intervals, until the morsels and shortening can be stirred into a smooth sauce.

Using a fork, dip the balls completely into the melted chocolate. Scrape gently on the side of the bowl or shake gently to remove any excess chocolate, then return to the baking sheet. Put cocoa or nut "dust" in a small strainer and tap over the truffles. Refrigerate for 30 minutes or until set before serving. Store in a tightly covered container in the refrigerator.

Yield: 36 truffles

Nestlé Toll House Truffles

Chocolate Chip Cookie Brittle

This is adapted from a popular microwave peanut brittle recipe on www.allrecipes.com. Make sure you measure out all the ingredients before starting the recipe.

1½ cups chopped walnuts
1 cup granulated sugar
½ cup light corn syrup
Pinch salt
1 tablespoon butter
1 teaspoon vanilla extract
½ teaspoon baking soda
1 cup (6 ounces) semisweet chocolate chips

Spray a baking sheet, the spout of a 4-cup glass measuring cup, and a spatula with nonstick cooking spray. Combine the walnuts, sugar, corn syrup, and salt in the measuring cup. Microwave for 6 to 7 minutes on high; the mixture should be bubbly and the walnuts should be golden brown (not burnt!). Stir in the butter and vanilla and microwave for 2 to 3 more minutes.

Quickly stir in the baking soda, just until the mixture is foamy. Pour immediately onto the baking sheet. Use the spatula or forks to quickly spread the mixture out evenly. When cool but still not completely set (5 to 10 minutes), evenly sprinkle the top of the candy with the chocolate chips. Wait another 5 minutes or until set. Break into pieces, and store in an airtight container.

Yield: 1 pound candy
Note: These directions are for a 700-watt microwave; the power and/or cooking times will need to be adjusted for higher-wattage ovens.

Chocolate Chip Cookie Mix in a Jar

Gingham-decorated jarred cookie mixes became the church bazaar rage a few years back, blowing away the poodle toilet paper holders and dish towel angel competition. This recipe is courtesy of Nestlé®.

1¾cups all-purpose flour
¾ teaspoon baking soda
¾ teaspoon salt
1½ cups (9 ounces) Nestlé Toll House® Semi-Sweet Chocolate Morsels
¾ cup packed brown sugar
½ cup granulated sugar

Combine the flour, baking soda, and salt in small bowl. Place the flour mixture in a 1-quart jar. Layer the remaining ingredients in the order listed above, pressing firmly after each layer. Seal with the lid and decorate with fabric and ribbon.

Preheat the oven to 375 degrees. Using an electric mixer, beat ¾ cup (1½ sticks) softened butter or margarine, 1 large egg, and ¾ teaspoon vanilla extract in a large bowl until blended. Add the cookie mix and ½ cup chopped nuts (optional); mix well, breaking up any clumps. Drop by rounded tablespoonfuls onto ungreased baking sheets. Bake for 9 to 11 minutes or until golden brown. Let cool on the baking sheets for 2 minutes; transfer to wire racks to cool completely.

Yield: 24 cookies.

Lollipop Chocolate Chip Cookies

The chocolate chip cookie as token gift: gussied up with ribbon and put on a stick. Lollipop sticks, cellophane, and ribbon are available at craft stores.

1 (16.5-ounce) package refrigerated chocolate chip cookie dough or ½ recipe Original Nestlé® Toll House® Chocolate Chip Cookies (page 123), unbaked

8 (5- to 6½-inch) lollipop sticks

Cellophane and ribbon (optional)

Preheat the oven to the temperature specified in the recipe or dough package. Shape the cookie dough into eight 2-inch balls. Evenly space the lollipop sticks on two ungreased baking sheets, four per sheet. Center a dough ball on the end of each stick and flatten the dough around it make a disk about ½ inch thick. Bake until the edges and tops begin to turn light brown, 13 to 15 minutes. Place the sheets on racks and let the cookies cool completely. Cover with cellophane and decorate with ribbon, if desired.

Lollipop Chocolate Chip Cookies

Yield: 8 lollipops

Carob Chip Dog Cookies

I offer this for those chocolate chip cookie lovers who are also dog lovers, and because this product is out there. But I think most dogs would prefer a big hunk of liver. *Note: Do not substitute regular chocolate chips for the carob.*

¾ cup water
¼ cup honey
¼ cup safflower oil
1 teaspoon vanilla extract
1½ cups oat flour
1½ cups whole-wheat flour
1 cup carob chips

Preheat the oven to 300 degrees. Combine the water, honey, oil, and vanilla in a medium bowl. Gradually add the oat flour and whole-wheat flour and mix until it forms a dough. (Add additional water if necessary.) Fold in the carob chips. Roll the dough into 1-inch balls and place on an ungreased baking sheet. Flatten the balls into cookie-like rounds. Bake 18 to 22 minutes or until the edges are golden brown. Cool. Place in a covered container. Store in the refrigerator for up to 3 months or the freezer for as long as 6 months.

Yield: 30 cookies

A Chip Primer

The chocolate chip cookie's very identity rests on the chip. Chips were actually invented to make this cookie. So what are they exactly?

Chocolate chips are basically cocoa solids, cocoa butter, and sugar—or the same ingredients in the candy bar chocolate that was originally cut up to use in the cookies, except that chips usually also contain emulsifiers to make them hold their shape, and less cocoa butter (because cocoa butter makes the chocolate more melty).

As to why that shape is not actually a chip: The teardrop is the most efficient way to create a small bite of chocolate in a chocolate factory, says Jane Hardman, director of technical applications for Nestlé® Baking. They're created when a pre-measured amount of liquid chocolate is deposited from a nozzle above a conveyor belt. "When the nozzle pulls back up, the chocolate curls," Hardman says.(Square-shaped chocolate chunks or bars must be made in rectangular molds and then cut, resulting in wasteful and messy shards.)

Ruth Wakefield's original Toll House® recipe called for semisweet chocolate but today the terms "semisweet," "bittersweet," and "dark" are used almost interchangeably. The key to the differences in quality and taste has to do with the cocoa beans and the way they are processed as well as the final total percentage of chocolate (cacao) and sugar in the chip. The cacao content of most mainstream supermarket brands of semisweet chips is in the 40s, whereas upscale brands of bittersweet chips made by Ghirardelli and Scharffen Berger have about 60 percent cacao.

A 2009 taste test by *Cook's Illustrated* rated Ghirardelli and Hershey tops. In 2010, the website Serious Eats liked Trader Joe's, Scharffen Berger, and Callebaut (in that order). American Culinary Institute chefs, the Copley News Service, and cookbook author Dorie Greenspan all favor Guittard, and regular Nestlé semisweet ranked number one with testers at the *Columbus Dispatch* and Food Network mad scientist Alton Brown.

In other words, the best chip to use is a matter of personal taste, although many high-end commercial bakers today hand-cut a lower-sugar, higher-cacao bar chocolate of their own choosing in place of any chip. This is both for the contrast it provides to the Toll House's sugary dough and because they actually like the way chocolate not formulated for a cookie will melt and infuse every bite.

Is it possible to have too many chips in a chocolate chip cookie? Yes. More than half of people surveyed by Nestlé said that six to 10 morsels per standard 2-inch chocolate chip cookie was ideal. Only 12 percent wanted 20 or more.

For her *Essential Chocolate Chip Cookbook*, Elinor Klivans experimented to find out how many chips cookie dough could comfortably hold. Her conclusion? Four cups of chips per 2 cups of dough (or the amount produced by half of the page 123 standard Toll House recipe). That equals 50 chips per cookie, or four times more than is recommended even by motivated chocolate chip makers.

Have It Your Way

Ruth Wakefield's Toll House® cookie recipe was great in its one-size-fits-all day, but in this era of almost limitless choice and even more information, a great recipe is only great if it's great to you. Fortunately this same proliferation of information online and on TV and availability of ingredients in supermarkets makes it easy to adapt her basic recipe to make your preferred chocolate chip cookie, whether it be crispy, cakey, or chewy. Below are some recipes to yield these types of cookies, along with general guidelines should you want to do your own fine-tuning.

Crisp Chocolate Chip Cookies

2¼ cups all-purpose flour

1 teaspoon baking soda

1 teaspoon salt

1 cup (2 sticks) butter, softened

1½ cups granulated sugar

½ cup packed brown sugar

1 teaspoon vanilla extract

1 large egg, room temperature

1½ tablespoons water

2 cups (12 ounces) semisweet chocolate chips

1 cup chopped nuts

Preheat the oven to 375 degrees. Grease two baking sheets. Combine the flour, baking soda and salt in a small bowl. Using an electric mixer, beat the butter, granulated sugar, brown sugar, and vanilla extract in a large bowl until creamy. Add the egg and water. Gradually beat in the flour mixture. Stir in the chocolate chips and nuts. Drop by rounded tablespoonfuls onto the baking sheets. Bake for 13 to 16 minutes or until golden brown. Let cool on baking sheets for 2 minutes; transfer to wire racks to cool completely.

Yield: 36 dozen cookies

Cakey Chocolate Chip Cookies

2¼ cups cake flour (or 2½ cups all-purpose flour)
2 tablespoons cornstarch
1½ teaspoons baking powder
1 teaspoon salt
1 cup vegetable shortening (preferably butter-flavored)
½ cup granulated sugar
1 cup packed brown sugar
2 teaspoons vanilla extract
3 large eggs, cold
2 cups (12 ounces) semisweet chocolate chips
1 cup chopped nuts

Preheat the oven to 375 degrees. Combine the flour, cornstarch, baking powder and salt in small bowl. Using an electric mixer, beat the butter, granulated sugar, brown sugar and vanilla extract in a large bowl until creamy. Add the eggs, one at a time, beating lightly after each addition. Gradually beat in the flour mixture. Stir in the chocolate chips and nuts. Cover the bowl with plastic wrap and refrigerate for at least 2 hours and preferably overnight.

Drop by rounded tablespoonfuls onto ungreased baking sheets. Bake 12 to 15 minutes or until golden brown. Let cool on the baking sheets for 2 minutes; transfer to wire racks to cool completely.

Yield: 36 cookies

Chewy Chocolate Chip Cookies

2¼ cups bread flour (or 2 cups all-purpose flour)
1 teaspoon baking soda
1 teaspoon salt
¾ cup (1½ sticks) butter, melted
2 tablespoons corn syrup
¼ cup granulated sugar
1¼ cup packed brown sugar
2 teaspoons vanilla extract
1 large egg plus 1 large yolk
2 cups (12 ounces) semisweet chocolate chips

Preheat the oven to 365 degrees. Combine the flour, baking soda, and salt in a small bowl. Using an electric mixer, beat the melted butter, corn syrup, granulated sugar, brown sugar, and vanilla extract in a large bowl until creamy. Add the egg and egg yolk. Gradually beat in the flour mixture. Stir in the chocolate chips. Drop by rounded tablespoonfuls onto ungreased baking sheets. Bake for 13 to 15 minutes or until golden brown. Let cool on the baking sheets for 2 minutes; transfer to wire racks to cool completely.

Yield: 36 cookies

General Principles of Crispy, Cakey, and Chewy

For thin, crispy cookies

- Keep all the ingredients at room temperature.
- Use butter instead of shortening or margarine and increase the amount by up to ½ cup.
- Blend the wet ingredients thoroughly.
- Use lots more granulated sugar than brown sugar.
- Add extra baking soda.
- Bake the cookies longer and/or increase the oven temperature.
- Substitute water or milk for one—or all—of the eggs.
- Cut down on the flour a little bit.
- Grease your baking sheets and don't let them cool completely between batches.

For soft, cakey cookies

- Work with chilled ingredients and chill the dough for at least 24 hours before baking.
- Use margarine or shortening instead of or in addition to butter. (Butter-flavored has beaten out butter in some blind tastings of chocolate chip cookies.)
- Increase the ratio of brown sugar to granulated sugar.
- Add an extra egg.
- Don't overbeat.
- Use nuts.
- Use cake flour or at least a little extra all-purpose flour.
- Use baking powder instead of baking soda.
- Keep the cookies small.
- Don't grease the baking sheets and let them cool between batches.
- Store these cookies in an air-tight container with a piece of bread or an apple slice.

For chewy cookies

- Melt the butter.
- Use bread flour or a little less all-purpose flour.
- Add an egg yolk for every egg called for in the recipe. Or substitute 3 tablespoons milk for one egg.
- Add 1 tablespoon corn syrup, honey, or molasses and reduce the sugar and any other liquid in the recipe accordingly.
- Reduce the baking temperature and/or baking time.
- Use mostly brown sugar.

For thicker cookies

- Reduce the butter by up to half.
- Increase the flour up to half a cup.
- Increase the baking temperature by 25 degrees and shorten the baking time by 10 minutes.
- Chill or even freeze the dough before baking.

For browner cookies

- Use mostly brown sugar and substitute 1 to 2 tablespoons corn syrup or molasses for some sugar.
- Use butter instead of shortening.

For cookies with multiple textures

- Make them bigger—dole the dough out with an ice cream scoop versus Ruth Wakefield's suggested teaspoonfuls.
- Freeze the dough before baking so the cookie stays somewhat soft inside.

Note: All specific amounts apply to recipes yielding 36 cookies.

Yet Another Reason to Get on the iWagon

The recipes and accompanying guidelines are great if all you're looking for is a cakey, chewy, or crisp chocolate chip cookie. But what if you want a chewy cookie that is also thick and crisp or a soft cookie that is thin and crumbly?

There's an app for that and it's called Cookulus (ends like calculus): Ultimate Chocolate Chip Cookie version for iPad and iPhone. It automatically adjusts the ingredient amounts, baking temperature, and time on a basic chocolate chip cookie recipe to meet your preferences on three graduated scales (chewy/crumbly, soft/crisp, and thick/thin) as well as for serving size and preferred type of measurement. The resulting instructions can be unorthodox—e.g. baking cookies for 45 minutes at 260 degrees—but in his late 2010 test *Washington Post* food writer Joe Yonan said Cookulus "worked like a charm" to create the very soft, very chewy, somewhat thin chocolate chip cookies of his dreams.

Cookulus: Ultimate Chocolate Chip Cookie app, including classic, chocolate chocolate chip, walnut, and whole wheat variations, was available at the iTunes store at press time for 99 cents. A more limited trial Soft & Chewy Chocolate Chip Cookie app is free.

Toll House® Tips and Tricks

Choosing the right chocolate isn't the only way you can improve your chocolate chip cookie. Here are other things to do that can make a big difference in quality:

- Toast your nuts to increase the flavor. To do that, spread them evenly on a baking sheet and place in a low oven (300 to 325 degrees) for 5 to 10 minutes or until they give off an aroma and turn light golden brown, stirring frequently and watching them to prevent burning. Nuts can also be toasted in a dry skillet on the stovetop: Place over medium heat and stir constantly until they begin to smell (about 4 minutes). Make sure to let the nuts cool completely before chopping or using them in

Vanilla beans

a recipe. To get the nut flavor minus the lumpy texture some people don't like, grind them into a coarse meal in a food processor.

- If you're using butter, try browning at least some of it. This was one of the main suggestions in a June 2009, *Cook's Illustrated* article called "The Perfect Chocolate Chip Cookie," and it gives the cookie a greater caramel/toffee flavor. Cook the butter on the stovetop at medium-high heat for a couple of minutes beyond melting, stirring constantly, until it has a dark brown color and a nutty aroma.
- Use real vanilla—or not. Most bakers and all three of the 1970s cookie titans swear by real vanilla extract. Made from soaking vanilla beans in alcohol, real vanilla does have a more complex flavor profile than imitation. But *Cook's Illustrated*'s 2009 vanilla extract taste test says almost all those added flavors get burned off in the high heat used to bake cookies. Imitation vanilla's vanillin may be created differently and less appetizingly (from wood pulp), but in cookies it performs just as well and for a fraction of real vanilla's cost, *CI*'s writers say. (Not convinced? To make your own real vanilla: Split two to four vanilla beans lengthwise, scrape out the insides, cut into 3-inch pieces, and then place in a clean, closed container with a cup of high-proof vodka, rum, or bourbon in a dark corner for at least a month—up to six months for the best flavor—shaking the bottle occasionally.)
- Use a flour with a reliable protein content. The protein content—or water-absorption abilities—of all-purpose flour can vary widely. Individual bags of a single brand can vary by almost 3 percent, says food science writer Shirley O. Corriher in her 2008 book *BakeWise*; this is especially true of store brands although it can occur in major national brands, too. And since lower-protein flours produce tenderer cookies with greater spread, and higher-protein ones make for coarser

How to Talk Like a Chocolate Chip Insider

Americans in the chocolate chip cookie business talk about the size of chocolate chips in relation to the number in a pound. Thus, a standard Nestlé® Toll House® morsel is 900 count; Nestlé Toll House Chunks are 500; and Toll House mini morsels, 5,000. Chips in standard supermarket-aisle cookies are typically about 2,000-count size.

Celebrity Chef Chocolate Chip Cookie Recipes: Nothing Really New Since 1938

"I potentially could have had 70 chocolate chip cookie recipes," says Tracey Zabar of her book, *One Sweet Cookie*, for which she solicited favorite cookie recipes from celebrity chefs. Yes, famous chefs and cookbook authors are as into chocolate chip cookies as the rest of us and as sure that their recipe is the best. "In the category of 'Great Chocolate Chip Cookie Recipes,' these get my vote for the greatest," Dorie Greenspan says in *Baking: From My Home to Yours*. "I couldn't imagine chocolate chip cookies tasting any better," David Lebovitz similarly boasts in *Ready for Dessert*.

But are their recipes really that different and better? I recently went through some cookbooks and articles to see and was astonished at how closely most of them stick to Ruth Wakefield's recipe.

Following is a list of the very few significant changes these famous chefs have made to this even more famous recipe. (Note: I do not consider a quarter teaspoon or quarter cup more or less than Toll House® significant.)

Maida Heatter in ***Great Chocolate Desserts***: Adds a teaspoon of vanilla and 4 more ounces of chocolate chips.

Amy Sedaris in ***I Like You: Entertaining Under the Influence***: Adds a teaspoon of vanilla and 6 more ounces of chocolate chips.

Dorie Greenspan in ***Baking: From My Home to Yours***: Doubles the vanilla.

Nick Malgieri in ***Cookies Unlimited***: Doubles the chocolate chips.

Thomas Keller in ***Ad Hoc at Home:*** *Family* ***Style Recipes***: Suggests using molasses sugar for brown and calls for 10 ounces of hand-cut bittersweet chocolate (half 55 percent cacao and half 70 to 72 percent).

Alice Medrich in ***Alice Medrich's Cookies and Brownies***: Melts the butter.

David Lebovitz in ***Ready for Dessert***: Increases the chocolate by 2 ounces and uses hand-chopped bittersweet or semisweet chocolate rather than chips; doubles the amount of (toasted) nuts; and suggests shaping the dough into logs to create uniformly sized cookies.

Pichet Ong of Spot Dessert Bar in ***One Sweet Cookie***: Adds 1⅓ cup unsweetened coconut and 1 cup chocolate (in pistole form).

Emeril Lagasse in ***There's a Chef in My Soup***: Includes white and milk as well as semisweet chips and (optional) toasted walnuts.

Craig Claiborne with ***Pierre Franey*** in the March 9, 1980, *New York* ***Times***: No significant changes.

Joanne Chang in *Flour: Spectacular Recipes from Boston's Flour Bakery + Café*: Substitutes 1 cup bread flour for 1 cup of all-purpose, and swaps in 3 ounces of milk chocolate for semisweet.

Amy Scherber and ***Toy Kim Dupree*** in ***The Sweeter Side of Amy's Bread***: Substitute an egg yolk for one of the eggs; add ¼ teaspoon ground ginger and 1 tablespoon molasses.

White House pastry chef Bill Yosses in ***The Perfect Finish***: Adds ¼ cup Nutella, subtracts 1 stick of butter and substitutes 1 split and scraped vanilla bean for the vanilla extract.

Matt Lewis and **Renato Poliafito in *Baked: New Frontiers in Baking***: Add ⅔ cup chocolate chips.

and chewier cookies, the bag you use can have a major effect on how your cookies turn out. That makes buying brand name flours with consistent protein content, like King Arthur (higher, at about 12 percent protein) and White Lily and Martha White (lower, at 8 or 9 percent), worth seeking out and paying more for. (Pillsbury and Gold Medal aim for a middle-of-the-road 10.5 percent, but according to Corriher, don't always hit it.)

- Really whip the wet ingredients together—at least five minutes. (*Cook's Illustrated* suggests doing this in several stages, and letting the mixture rest for several minutes between mixings.) Conversely, once you add the flour, be gentle and don't overmix.
- Rotate your baking sheet front to back halfway through the bake time to even out oven hot spots that all ovens have. Bake only one sheet at a time, ideally.

Department of So, Do We Look Like We Care?

In six months of 1993 surrounding the introduction of detailed Nutrition Facts labels on packaged foods, consumption of chocolate chip cookies increased by 10 percent.

The Cookie Artist

In *101 Perfect Chocolate Chip Cookies*, Gwen Steege suggests melting 1 of the 2 cups of chocolate chips called for in a standard recipe in a saucepan on the stove or in a microwave. After folding in the chips, carefully stir in the melted chocolate just enough to create stripes but not so much that it blends into the dough.

And to make the Half and Half cookies pictured on the cover of *A Baker's Field Guide to Chocolate Chip Cookies*, Dede Wilson combines half of the cookie dough made with a fairly standard 2-cup-flour chocolate chip cookie recipe with 3 tablespoons cocoa and a cup of white chocolate chips; the other half gets a cup of semisweet. Then she squishes teaspoons of each of these doughs together before baking so that the cookie ends up half brown and half tan.

At the very least you might want to consider reserving half a cup of the chocolate chips called for in the standard recipe and using them to decorate the top of each cookie so people are aware of all the great chocolate they will be eating. (Mrs. Fields used to actually discard cookies where the chips weren't clearly visible.)

Cheat Sheet of Many Cookies

It would be possible to have a whole chapter of chocolate chip cookie recipes—nay, an entire chocolate chip cookie cookbook—that consists of nothing but minor variations on the basic Toll House® theme. Possible, but a waste of valuable ink and paper when I'm sure you are perfectly capable of turning back to page 123 for the basic Toll House recipe and then tweaking it per the below instructions to create these famous (and in some cases, infamous) variations. Note that this listing adheres to this chapter's laser-like focus on the Toll House taste, thus explaining the omission of such extreme flavor-changers as peanut butter and cocoa powder.

Bacon CCC: Add ½ pound bacon, cooked and chopped into ½-inch pieces, and use ½ cup of the rendered bacon fat (chilled to a solid in the fridge) for half of the called-for butter.

Ice Cream Sundae CCC

Brussels Sprouts CCC: Add ¼ cup flour, ½ cup sugar, and 2 cups of boiled, drained, and chopped fresh Brussels sprouts.

Candy CCC: Add up to 2 cups of your favorite candy bar, chopped up.

Caramel CCC: Add 1 to 2 cups caramel candies (cut into ¼-inch dice) or caramel baking bits.

Cereal CCC: Add up to 4 cups of your favorite cereal—up to 4 cups of a light cereal like Rice Krispies and more like ¾ to 1 cup for heavier, denser ones like Grape-Nuts or oatmeal (anything except instant).

Coffee CCC: Add 4 tablespoons double-strength freshly brewed coffee, the same amount of Kahlua or instant coffee, or 2 teaspoons instant espresso powder.

Donut CCC: Add 6 cups finely chopped glazed doughnuts (about eight doughnuts).

Fiber-Powered CCC: Substitute whole-wheat flour or barley for some or all of the all-purpose flour and/or throw in ½ cup wheat germ.

Heath CCC: Swap out 1 cup of chopped Heath Bar candy for 1 cup of chocolate chips.

Hippy CCC: Add ¼ cup sesame seeds and ½ cup sunflower kernels or hulled, toasted pumpkin seeds.

Ice Cream Sundae CCC: Add 2 cups broken sugar ice cream cones (about eight cones) and ¾ cup dried and chopped maraschino cherries.

Mint CCC: Add 1 teaspoon peppermint extract.

Orange CCC: Add 1 teaspoon to 1 tablespoon grated orange peel or candied orange peel and/or 1 teaspoon orange extract or Grand Marnier.

Sandwich CCC: Slather the flat side of a cookie with caramel sauce, frosting, equal parts blended cream cheese and marshmallow creme, Nutella, fruit spread, or ice cream and top with a second cookie.

Spicy CCC: Use half the called-for vanilla and add 3 to 4 drops hot pepper sauce, or ½ to 1 teaspoon cayenne or chipotle chili powder and the same amount of ground cinnamon.

Tipsy CCC: Add 1 teaspoon whiskey or 4 tablespoons stout beer.

Wasabi Ginger CCC: Add 2 teaspoons wasabi powder and 4 teaspoons ground ginger and use white instead of semisweet chips.

Chocolate Chip Cookie Nutrition:

The Bad News

The 5-inch chocolate chip cookies produced by David Leite's *New York Times* recipe with added traditional Toll House® walnuts contain 485 calories and 30 grams of fat (each!).

The Good News

Walnuts are extremely high in omega-3 fatty acids, which have been shown to protect against heart disease and stroke. In fact, in one study, participants who ate only four walnuts a day—or about the number that would be in one of these 5-inch cookies—had increased levels of these heart-healthy fatty acids for several weeks.

More Good News

The high-cacao dark chocolate used in the *New York Times* cookie recipe and most chocolate chip cookies made by high-end bakeries are high in antioxidants that can block free-radical action that has been linked to cancer, cardiovascular disease, Parkinson's and Alzheimer's. These benefits have been seen in people who eat as little as 3.5 ounces of 60- to 70-percent cacao dark chocolate a day (or about the amount in two and half of the *New York Times* cookies—but hey, it's for your health!).

More Bad News

Milk appears to negate dark chocolate's positive antioxidant effect. In other words, forget about that tall glass of cold milk (and its great calcium and Vitamin D) and consider instead washing that chocolate chip cookie down with a cup of antioxidant-rich black coffee or tea.

Next Up: A Study on How People Like Being Let Off Work Early

"Our study found that people preferred chocolate chip cookies that were made using a traditional fat. . . . Cookies made with [a] fat replacement [like prune paste] were rated as significantly less desirable than those made with a traditional fat."
—from "The Effect of Fat Replacement on Sensory Attributes of Chocolate Chip Cookies" by O. Charlton and M. K. Sawyer-Morse in the *Journal of the American Dietetic Association,* Dec. 1996

6

Celebrating Chocolate Chip Cookies

It's one thing to make and eat and even talk about a foodstuff; even broccoli gets that much attention. Eats that inspire festivals, teleplays, acting, jokes, cartoons—even crime—by contrast, are special and few. Chocolate chip cookies are such a food. In this chapter, I explore the consequences of chocolate chip cookie love and obsession.

Making the world's largest cookie

Monster Accomplishment

In the early 1990s, Scott Blackwell's Immaculate Consumption coffee shop was known for its pancake-sized chocolate chip cookies. But they were a little snack compared to the 102-foot, 38,000-pound chocolate chipper he and the team at Immaculate Baking Company made on May 17, 2003, setting a still-standing Guinness World Record for largest cookie.

By the late 1990s, Immaculate had morphed from coffee shop to one of the most successful lines of all-natural packaged cookies in the country and owner Blackwell was ready to give back. Specifically he was looking to raise money for a foundation to support the folk artists he admired and hired to decorate his cookie packaging. He also wanted to bring the title for world's largest chocolate chip cookie, then held by a New Zealand company, back to the cookie's American birthplace. (Join with me now in the Immaculate fight song: Go, go, chocolate chip! U.S.A! U.S.A!)

It should be noted that Blackwell made this declaration before he knew the size of the New Zealand cookie (87 feet) or Guinness's requirements (for a cookie of a uniform thickness baked in a single piece, rather than in sections).

The effort consumed nine months of planning, testing, and discarding of such crazy ideas as laying the dough with an asphalt-paving machine and baking it with a heat-blasting golf cart. They finally decided to build a convection-style oven consisting of a giant metal pizza pan surrounded by propane heaters and covered with the kind of material used for helium balloons (to trap the heat). A machine used to make building tile was modified to make slabs of cookie dough (after a good scrubbing, natch!).

It was a great plan until two days

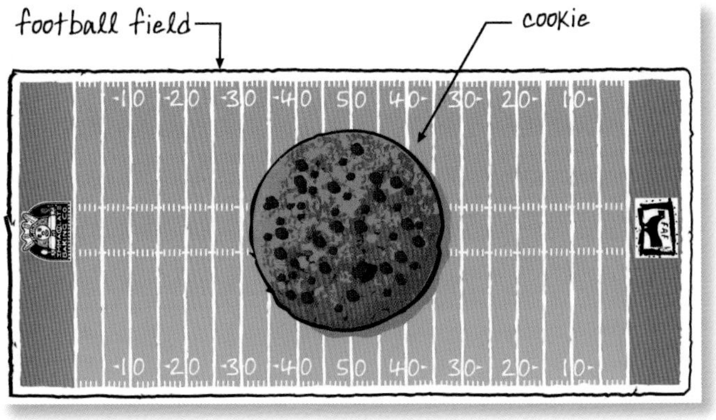

Relative size of the world's largest cookie

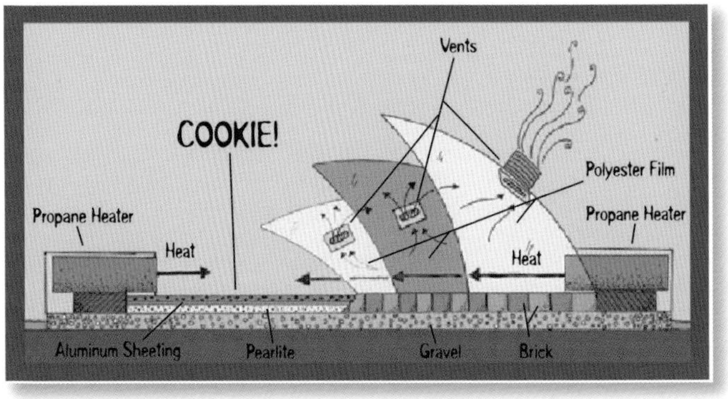

How the world's largest cookie's oven worked

before the scheduled bake date, when heavy winds threatened to rip the film cover off the pan and the project's engineer ordered it removed—10 minutes before a huge thunderstorm blew in and filled the metal pan with water. The oven was now in the running to be the world's largest metal swimming pool. The world's largest cookie team's spirits were similarly dampened until Blackwell gave a win-one-for-the-Gipper speech, and volunteers from the community who heard of the cookie crisis showed up with buckets and mops and rags and dried the pan off.

And after six hours of dough-laying and seven more of baking, the world's largest cookie was cut up and sold, producing enough of the other kind of dough to start the Folk Artist's Foundation (www.helpfaf.org).

World's Largest Cookie's Ingredients

Should you want to beat Immaculate's record, you will need more than:
12,200 pounds flour
6,525 pounds butter
6,000 pounds (10 million) dark chocolate chunks
5,000 pounds sugar
3,370 pounds dark brown sugar
30,000 eggs
184 pounds salt
79 pounds baking soda
10 gallons vanilla extract

Preparing to bake the world's largest cookie

The cookie drop at Ripon's Cookie Daze festival

Previous attempts to bake the world's largest chocolate chip cookie include:

June 10, 1975: At the urging of some ninth-graders and after producing several giant burnt cookies, South Boston bakery owner David Freedman used pans of cold water to cool down his bread oven enough to produce one 8-foot, 175-pound chocolate chip monster. Ruth Wakefield herself was on hand to taste the result, which she called "more like a Toll House® brownie."

July 1985: Another 8-foot cookie attempt, this one at the Buttrey grocery store in Great Falls, Montana. Weighing 231 pounds, it was placed on a special reinforced Masonite cookie sheet that got caught on an oven roller until the oven temperature was lowered and one brave baker crawled inside and freed it.

July 11, 1992: Employees of Ripon Foods, makers of Rippin' Good Cookies, in Ripon, Wisconsin, and community volunteers armed with rolling pins took two hours to spread 3,500 pounds of cookie dough onto a 907-square-foot oven that revolved like a giant record player. Two and a half hours later, the cookie was cut into 8,163 pieces by a metal arm wielding multiple pizza cutters. Though they subsequently lost the Guinness "largest cookie" crown, the town still celebrates the accomplishment and its cookie-making heritage annually at Cookie Daze, a community festival highlighted by the moment when 9,000 individually wrapped cookies are dropped from the top of a fire truck ladder and into the waiting arms of hundreds of Ripon kids.

March 13, 2003: Bakers at Universal Studios Japan spent three days baking up a 11.5-foot-diameter, 1-foot-thick, 1.2-ton chocolate chip cookie to promote a new

4-D Movie Magic ride featuring Cookie Monster and the rest of the *Sesame Street* gang.

Sweet Temptation

The triple sirens of semisweet chocolate, brown sugar, and crispy walnuts has led more than one chocolate chip cookie lover into a life of crime.

Consider the Boston-area postal employee who faced federal charges of destruction of mail in 1983 after he nibbled on the contents of a partly open package of irresistible chocolate chip cookies.

Or Fred Jackson of Detroit, sentenced to 11 years in prison in 1969 after he was caught climbing out of a grocery store window with five boxes of chocolate chip cookies (sprinkled with gold dust maybe?).

Or the similar, more recent, case of Kevin Weber, who got 26 years to life for stealing four restaurant cookies. That was, in part because of Weber's prior felonies and California's "three strikes and you're out" law. The real crime, to me? Weber was caught before he got to eat any.

Drug charges probably constitute the largest category of criminal prosecutions involving chocolate chip cookies. They are so wholesome and innocent, who would think you'd find drugs in there?

Certainly not the six members of a Tomahawk, Wisconsin, wedding party who got sick on the pot-laced chocolate chip cookies served to them in 1966 by the groom's brother, who was subsequently arrested. Comrade-in-spirit Krystina McDermott was arrested when police found crack cocaine in her bag of chocolate chip cookies during a routine traffic stop in El Paso in 2011.

You could argue that these desecrators of the chocolate chip cookie got what was coming. But what about 19-year-old Larry Wallick, who was arrested in 1977 for merely eating a chocolate chip cookie?

This was on Fire Island, New York, then apparently experiencing a tourist trash problem, addressed by a litter ordinance that prohibited public eating of any kind, whether or not littering was involved.

After a protest march by cookie fans wearing T shirts reading, COOKIES? YES! and more press than John Kerry got when he was running for president, the charges were dismissed on the grounds that the law was being unfairly applied to cookie lovers.

Reached at his college dorm on the day of the decision, Wallick expressed gratitude, both to the cookie store owner who paid for his lawyer and for the notoriety that prompted college classmates to bake him a batch of chocolate chip cookies.

They're Not Just for Eating

In addition to eating enjoyment, chocolate chip cookies have also been used:

- to thank Canadian diplomats who helped free six Americans during the 1980 Iranian hostage crisis.
- as *the* food subjects are asked to resist in numerous academic studies about diet and self control.
- to pop the question. In 1984 one customer of the Original Cookie Company in the Riverside Mall in North Utica, New York, asked an employee to write "Please say yes" on a giant cookie, before bringing his girlfriend round. (She accepted. Who wouldn't, with a lifetime of chocolate chip cookie eating in the offing?)
- in the form of frozen cookie dough, as a popular fundraiser for nonprofit groups. (They're a lot less work than car washes.)
- as the negotiating-table treat that got city and county representatives to stop arguing and start making some progress on an agreement for control of the Cincinnati waterfront in 1998. (Could somebody please deliver a truckload of cookies to the U.S. House and Senate?)
- to sell houses, baking up a batch to make a house smell like a home being a standard part of any decent real estate agent's bag of sales tricks.
- to recruit students. Hood College in 2010 handed out chocolate chip cookies made by an alum in the cookie business to prospective students as a bribe, first and foremost, but also as a way for them to see the important things "you can do with a Hood education," said college enrollment VP Kathleen Bands at the time.

They're Good Enough for Him

The Cookie Monster loves all cookies. But his favorite is chocolate chippies. He's said as much in several interviews (for www.uso.org in 2012 and on *Martha Stewart Living* in 2001), before *OMM, NOM-NOM-NOM*-ing some down.

If, as childhood development experts claim, the Cookie Monster is the furry blue monster

Cookie Monster

incarnation of the kids who watch him, then it makes sense that he should share kids' love of this variety as well as their single-minded desire to get them and everything else they want.

One somewhat disturbing behind-the-scenes fact about the chippies Cookie Monster eats on *Sesame Street* is revealed in David Borgenicht's *Sesame Street Unpaved*: Because the chocolate and oil in cookies can make a Muppet greasy, the Cookie Monster is actually eating rice cakes painted to look like chocolate chip cookies.

The light weight of the cakes is also good considering that Cookie Monster hovers over the head of the Muppeteer who voices him and so anything going into the big black hole that is Cookie Monster's mouth lands on top of the Muppeteer's head.

These cookies were an essential ingredient in the Got Milk? campaign.

Would You Like Milk with That?

Hitch your wagon to a star and you'll go far.

That's what milk makers did to the much more appealing chocolate chip cookies in 1993, and the result was one of the most successful advertising campaigns in history.

Almost since advertising started, milk ads have promoted the drink's many health benefits. Despite, or maybe because of this finger-wagging approach, milk consumption in America in the early '90s showed no signs of ending its 30-year slide.

Until 1993, when the California Milk Processor Board asked the Goodby, Berlin & Silverstein agency to create an ad campaign that instead focused on the more appealing foods people liked to drink milk with, like chocolate chip cookies.

One of the very first ads of that groundbreaking campaign showed a picture of a chocolate chip cookie with one bite taken out and the question, "Got Milk?" In happy-happy ad land, it was an unusual case of a campaign designed to make people imagine an unpleasant future and act to avoid it.

A popular television ad from the Got Milk? campaign's second phase showed a pompous executive firing someone on his cell phone while walking into the path of a speeding semi. Fade to black, and suddenly this guy is in an all-white kitchen, stuffing his face with the dozens of fresh-baked chocolate chip cookies. He opens a refrigerator to find dozens of milk cartons. But the first one he grabs is empty and so are all the others. And we and he suddenly realize he's not in heaven after all.

There were also Cookie Monster and Pillsbury Doughboy (see page 58) ads and even a Got Milk? Barbie that came complete with spotted cow costume and Nestlé® Toll House® cookie recipe.

The campaign was a win for both the California milk sellers, who saw sales increase 6.8 percent after years of declines, and the ad agency, which won more than 100 industry awards.

At least it was until late 2006, when the milk board decided to up the impact of chocolate chip cookie "Got Milk?" ads by placing chocolate chip cookie–scented strips in some San Francisco bus shelters—and complaints from people who apparently missed the usual exhaust fume and urine smells got them taken down.

Cookie Competition

The most popular thing to bake in America is also, not coincidentally, the most popular focus for single-food baking contests. Anyone who decides to hold one will find no shortage of entrants.

A young Beaver Creek Resort cookie contest competitor

"We were hoping for maybe 40 dozen, not 117 [dozen]," lamented Kris Schommer of Mayville, Wisconsin, radio station The Great 98 as she surveyed the plates of chocolate chips that covered every table in the building just two weeks after their contest was announced in 2004. In 2012, the Minnesota State Fair took the radical step of discontinuing its chocolate chip cookie contest both to cut down on work and in hopes of boosting interest in other cookie contest categories.

These contests are also popular with newspapers and as part of chocolate festivals. Fourteen-year-old Jordan Hall beat her grandmom Ann Hess at Fond du Lac, Wisconsin, Chocolate Fantasy's "Ultimate" Chocolate Chip Cookie Contest in 2009 with an entry tauntingly called Jordan's Better than Gramma's Chocolate Chip Cookies—although Hess got her revenge when she won in 2012. (See page 182 for another winning recipe from this contest.)

Ultimate Chocolate Chip Cookie Contest medal

You'll find the slopes wide open at the Beaver Creek Resort in Colorado most days at 3 pm. That's Cookie Time, when resort servers come out of the kitchen bearing trays of warm chocolate chip cookies—almost 2,000 daily—to give away free to guests. Their eight-year-old annual cookie competition, which attracted 106 entries and 2,000 eaters in 2011, celebrates that tradition.

Several of the largest and most famous past chocolate chip cookie contests were book-driven virtual events. Larry and Honey Zisman's two National Chocolate Chip Cookie contests drew a combined 11,500 recipes and yielded two cookbooks. The recipes in *The 37 Best Chocolate Chip Cookies in America* were culled from a contest sponsored by the Princeton, New Jersey-based American Reflections in 1980.

Chester Soling launched his 1987 chocolate chip cookie contest as a way to promote his Western Massachusetts Orchards Inn's then somewhat novel practice of serving guests fresh-baked chocolate chip cookies at bedtime. The book of 101 of the best of the 2,600 entries published several years later includes a recipe containing a can of pinto beans (thus raising the question of what might have been in the losing 2,499).

But smart contestants stick pretty close to Toll House®. In fact, judges for the *Huffington Post*'s *Kitchen Daily* spring 2012 chocolate chip cookie contest passed over entries containing pomegranate, flan, and whiskey in favor of a recipe which basically just upped the brown sugar and chocolate in Ruth Wakefield's recipe.

LIGHTS, CAMERA, COOKIES!

Probably the most famous television show or movie to feature chocolate chip cookies is a 2000 episode of the situation comedy, *Friends*, called "The One About Phoebe's Cookies." In it, the gang is trying to figure out what to get Monica and Chandler for an engagement present. Monica says she would really love Phoebe's grandmother's recipe for chocolate chip cookies, which Phoebe says she made a deathbed promise never to reveal. Phoebe eventually caves to Monica's pleas, only to discover that the recipe was lost in an apartment fire: All she has left is one cookie from her freezer that was made from the recipe. Monica spends most of the episode trying

A giant chocolate chip cookie presides over Beaver Creek's cookie contest awards ceremony (here shown with 2011 winner Shannon Bostrom).

Chocolate Chipees with a Caramel Puddle

A caramel center and chocolate drizzle elevated Lucy Mathers's award-winner from Fond du Lac, Wisconsin's 2011 Ultimate Chocolate Chip Cookie Contest above the competition and many other Toll House® riffs, while not requiring much more work than the standard recipe. Providing you choose your chocolate chips wisely, these cookies will also be vegan.

2¼ cups flour

1 teaspoon baking soda

1 teaspoon salt

½ cup nondairy margarine (such as Earth Balance), softened

½ cup butter-flavored Crisco

¾ cup packed brown sugar

¾ cup granulated sugar

2 teaspoons vanilla extract

1 tablespoon egg substitute that uses no egg product

2 tablespoons water

3 cups (18 ounces) chocolate chips

1 cup sweetened, flaked coconut (optional)

2 cups chopped pecans or peanuts

2 cups store-bought or homemade caramel topping

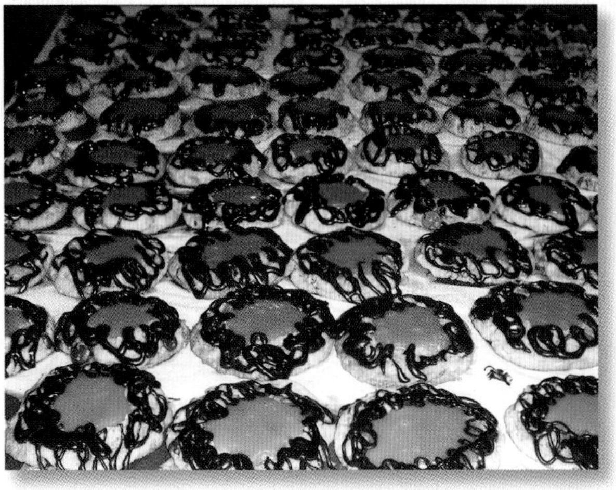

Chocolate Chipees with a Caramel Puddle

Preheat the oven to 350 degrees. Whisk together the flour, baking soda, and salt. Cream the Crisco, nondairy margarine, brown sugar, granulated, sugar, and vanilla. Mix the egg replacement with the water until foamy, then add to the creamed mixture. Stir the flour mixture into the sugar mixture. Stir in 2 cups of the chocolate chips and the coconut, if using. Chill. Shape the dough into 2-inch balls and roll each ball in the chopped nuts. Make a dent in the center of each ball. Bake on ungreased baking sheets for 10 minutes. Place the baking sheets on wire racks until the cookies are completely cool. Melt the remaining chocolate chips. Fill each indent with caramel topping, and drizzle melted chocolate over the cookies.

Yield: About 36 cookies

to recreate the recipe using that cookie as model, without much success. Pressed on whether there might not be someone else in the family who has the recipe, Phoebe suggests one of her French relatives, adding, "My grandmother says she got the recipe from her grandmother, Nesele Toulouse."

"What was her name?" Monica asks.

"Nesele Toulouse."

"Nestlé® Toll House®?" Monica yells, grabbing a yellow bag of Nestlé Toll House morsels and pointing to the recipe on the back. "Is this the recipe?"

"Yes!!" Phoebe says, finally realizing.

Says Monica, "I can't believe I just spent the last two days trying to figure out the recipe and it was in my cupboard the whole time!"

Before *The Simpsons* spun off as its own show, they were cartoon shorts that ran on Tracey Ullman's variety show, including in Ullman's second season in 1987, "The Perfect Crime." In the one-and-a-half-minute cartoon, Bart unsuccessfully tries to blame the wordless baby Maggie for missing chocolate chip cookies that he has stolen. The cartoon ends with Maggie leading Marge and Homer along a trail of crumbs to Bart, his belly swollen, writhing on the floor from his cookie pig-out.

Some other memorable chocolate chip on-screen moments:

In ***Clueless*** **(1995)**, a baking-clueless Cher (Alicia Silverstone), throws an uncut log of refrigerated cookie dough onto a baking sheet in anticipation of her big date with Christian (Justin Walker), declaring, "Whenever a boy comes, you should always have something baking."

In ***Home Alone 2: Lost in New York*** **(1992)**, the first thing Macaulay Culkin does after getting into his family's room at the Plaza is raid the in-room refrigerator of its chocolate chip cookies.

Peter Fonda and Susan St. James snack on a bag of Famous Amos chocolate chip cookies in ***Outlaw Blues*** **(1977)**.

An Unusual Suspect

The wholesome and innocent chocolate chip has been a culprit in several murder mysteries. Joanne Fluke launched her career as a mystery writer and her 15-book series featuring professional baker/amateur sleuth Hannah Swenson with *The Chocolate Chip Cookie Murder*. (And yes, her book signings do often feature baked goods.) And a major subplot of *The Big Bad City* (1989), the 49th title in famed mystery writer Ed McBain's 87th Precinct series, focuses on The Cookie Boy, a thief who leaves a box of chocolate chip cookies at the scene of each crime.

All-Grown-Up Chewy Chocolate Chip Cookies

Judges at the Best Darn Chocolate Chip Cookie Contest, held at the late, great Copa food and wine education center in Napa Valley, California, called this a cookie "with a complex flavor" and "strong chocolate punch" that "is not too sweet." It won third place and people's choice for Paige Isbutt in 2006. The first prize winner was a chocolate-chocolate chip cookie and therefore outside the scope of this book, if not of that contest.

1 cup (2 sticks) unsalted butter, room temperature
⅔ cup packed light brown sugar
½ cup granulated sugar
¼ cup golden syrup (preferably Lyle's)
1 large egg
1 tablespoon vanilla extract
¼ cup malted milk powder (preferably Carnation)
½ teaspoon instant espresso powder
2¼ cups all-purpose flour (preferably King Arthur unbleached)
1⅛ teaspoons salt
½ teaspoon baking powder
¼ teaspoon baking soda
1 pound bittersweet chocolate chips (preferably Ghirardelli 60 percent Bittersweet Baking Chips)

Adjust a rack to the middle position and preheat the oven to 375 degrees. Line baking sheets with parchment paper. In a large bowl, cream together the butter, brown sugar, granulated sugar, and golden syrup. Beat in the egg, vanilla, malted milk powder, and espresso powder. Add the flour, salt, baking powder, and baking soda; stir until thoroughly combined. Stir in the chocolate chips. Drop the dough by rounded tablespoonfuls (or use a small ice cream scoop) 3 inches apart onto the prepared baking sheets. Bake, one sheet at a time, for 10 to 11 minutes, until golden brown at the edges; the center will appear slightly undercooked. Transfer the sheet of baked cookies to a wire rack. Let cool for at least 10 minutes before removing the cookies from the parchment.

Yield: About 30 cookies

Celebrity Chipsters

When she was 15, Barbra Streisand played a chocolate chip as part of an acting exercise involving an inanimate object.

"I was stuck into a sticky batter, put into an oven where I swelled and started to melt and burn," she recalled in a 1970 *Life* magazine story. "I was taken out of the oven where the air congealed my outer layer, leaving my insides mushy. My head—meaning my point—started to droop when somebody ate me."

Chocolate chip cookies were never the same for her after that, she noted.

Actress Ashley Judd says baking chocolate chip cookies is her favorite way to de-stress. Country singer Trisha Yearwood's earliest cooking memory is of baking chocolate chip cookies with her mom. Other (nonpolitical) famous chocolate chip cookie fans include Diana Ross, Olivia Newton-John, Carol Burnett, Imelda Marcos, Cloris Leachman, Elton John, Ann-Margret, Rosie O'Donnell (who told me she grew up on New York's Linden's packaged) and indie-rock goddess Neko Case, who once told *Spin* magazine that she spent almost five years tweaking the Nestlé® Toll House® cookie recipe to her non-puffy preference. (See page 65 to learn about the cookie's many famous politician fans.)

A teenage Barbra Streisand onstage

Chocolate Chip Cookie Jokes 'n Riddles

Q: How do you know when a blonde has been making chocolate chip cookies?

A: There are M&M shells all over the floor.

Q: When does the chocolate chip cookie go to the doctor?

A: When it's feeling crummy.

Q: Why do basketball players love chocolate chip cookies?

A: Because they can dunk them.

Chocolate chip cookies are common fodder for comic strips, like this 1997 Peanuts.

Last Meal

A man lies dying upstairs in his bed. He smells the scent of his very favorite dessert baking in the kitchen downstairs. With all the strength he can muster, he gets out of bed, crawls down the stairs and staggers to the kitchen, where he sees a big plate of chocolate chip cookies cooling on the counter. But when he reaches for one, his wife slaps his hand away. "Those are for the funeral!" she angrily explains.

School Daze

Kids are lined up in a parochial school cafeteria for lunch. At the end of the line is a big bowl of apples, with a note attached reading, "Take only one. God is watching." A little further along is a big plate of chocolate chip cookies with another sign, in a student's scrawl, reading, "Take all you want. God is watching the apples."

A Political Joke

A union organizer, a Tea Partier and a CEO are sitting at a table in front of a plate with a dozen chocolate chip cookies. The CEO reaches over, swoops up 11 of them and says to the Tea Partier, "Watch out for that union guy: I think he wants a piece of your cookie."

Traveler's Treats

"Why a cookie?" was the question on the bag containing a chocolate chip cookie that DoubleTree hotel clerks have long handed out to every arriving guest.

Why indeed. You might think people would choose their hotels for their proximity to tourist attractions or the softness of their beds.

The problem, says brand expert Erich Joachimsthaler, is that people don't always know about these more substantive differences in available hotels and airlines.

In that case, "cookies can create meaningful differentiation," Joachimsthaler says. Especially meaningful in the case of cookies, which are, the DoubleTree bag went on to explain, "warm, personal, and inviting, much like our hotels and the staff here that serves you."

The DoubleTree cookie tradition began in the early 1980s as a perk for VIPS offered by just a few of the hotels, but which was eventually embraced by the entire company in a big way. In 2002, DoubleTree's VP of marketing traveled to Minneapolis to personally hand over the chain's 100 millionth free cookie. In 2011, DoubleTree celebrated the 25th anniversary of the tradition by sending a "care-van" to 50 U.S. cities to give cookies away. DoubleTree also gives out free cookies randomly at every hotel opening and on every Fourth of July. No wonder they've become known as "the cookie hotel."

The cookie dough is made by the Christie Cookie Company in Nashville (see page 113), flash-frozen and then baked at the hotels several times a day and kept in warming drawers built into DoubleTree's reception desks. About half of guests start eating their cookie right there in the lobby; half wait until just after they get into their rooms, the Times Square New York DoubleTree hotel manager told the *New York Times* in early 2010. How does he know? Because the first thing most guests do when they get into their room of that high-rise is go to the window and look at the view and his hotel is constantly having to launder the curtains to remove "the chocolate fingerprints."

A DoubleTree Hotel guest gets his cookie

DoubleTree Hotel-Like Cookies

No trips planned? The following recipe is based on some by ex-DoubleTree employees as well as a careful reading of the ingredient list on the DoubleTree cookie bag. People who like the way the cookies are presented at the DoubleTree (already made!) as much as the actual cookies can also order them from DoubleTree cookie maker Christie Cookie at www.doubletreecookies.com or 800-916-0097.

1½ cups all-purpose flour
¾ cup malted barley flour
½ cup quick-cooking oats
1½ teaspoons baking soda
1 teaspoon salt
¼ teaspoon cinnamon
1 cup butter, softened
¾ cup packed brown sugar
¾ cup granulated sugar
2 large eggs
2 teaspoons vanilla extract
½ teaspoon lemon juice
3 cups semisweet chocolate chips (preferably Ghirardelli)
1½ cups chopped walnuts

DoubleTree Cookie

Line baking sheets with parchment paper. In a medium bowl, combine the all-purpose flour, barley malt flour, oats, baking soda, salt, and cinnamon. Using an electric mixer, beat the butter in a large bowl until creamy. Add the brown sugar and granulated sugar and beat on medium speed for about 2 minutes. Add the eggs, one at a time, beating well after each addition. Add the vanilla and lemon juice and mix well. Add the flour mixture to the butter mixture and stir well to blend. Stir in the chocolate chips and walnuts with a wooden spoon. Refrigerate the dough for at least 3 hours or as long as overnight. (If you're in a hurry, you can scoop the dough, then place it in a freezer for 20 minutes.)

Preheat the oven to 350 degrees. Using a ¼-cup measure or a 2-ounce ice cream scoop, drop the batter on the prepared pans, leaving 2 to 3 inches between each cookie. Bake for 13 to 18 minutes or until lightly browned around the edges but still soft in the middle. Let cool in the pans for about 5 minutes, then transfer cookies to wire racks.

Yield: About 24 cookies

Midwest Airlines is another travel business that became famous for its chocolate chip cookies. It was the result of a Midwest commissary employee's experiments to see what foods could be successfully cooked in the on-board ovens. Pizza rolls and popcorn were flops but the smell from cookies in the enclosed space was so great that a hungry member of the flight crew came out to investigate. (Fortunately, this guy was not flying the plane at the time.)

By 1986, Midwest was serving two free warm cookies to passengers on every flight after 10 am. It became so much a part of the airline's identity that the website the airline launched to combat a takeover attempt by AirTran in 2007 was the prescient www.savethecookie.com. Although the cookie survived that threat, it went the way of hot stewardesses and ample leg room under new owner Frontier in 2012.

Acknowledgments

My mom first introduced me to the chocolate chip cookie. Though the best (really, Mom!), she turns out to be only the first of many people who so generously shared their knowledge and love of this cookie with me.

I feel lucky to have embarked on this project within the lifetimes of people who knew chocolate chip cookie inventor Ruth Wakefield. I am particularly grateful for information and insights provided by her daughter, Mary Jane, and Ruth's friends, employees, business associates, and customers herein named, especially Marguerite Gaquin, Carol Cavanagh, Donald and Carol Saccone, and June O'Leary (who provided links to the also-invaluable John Campbell and Mary Alice Kirby). Other helpful Bay Staters include Neil and Vicki-Ann Downing, Todd Vetter, Nicole Casper, Dorothy Hogan-Schofield, Carolyn Ravenscroft, Theresa and Brina Healy, Daniel Freedman, Adele Blumenkrantz, Ana Silfer, and Donna Halper. Colleen Previte at Framingham State University (Ruth's alma mater) and writer Arthur Lubow were particularly helpful in tracking down the real story of the cookie's invention.

This project literally would not have been possible without the cooperation of Nestlé®, the company which Ruth entrusted with her cookie recipe and which nurtures her beloved Toll House® brand to this day. For several days in spring 2012 at the Nestlé Toll House headquarters in Solon, Ohio, and in dozens of subsequent phone and email conversations, Roz O'Hearn, Jim Coyne, Jenny Harper, and Stephen Lan opened their minds and files to me in ways that benefited this book immeasurably. Ditto for their slightly less Wyman-burdened colleagues Jane Hardman, Susan Geringer, Kelly Malley, Daryl Mummery, and Tracey Gibb.

I was also fortunate to get interviews, photos, and/or recipes from all the important past and present chocolate chip and chocolate chip cookie makers. Thanks to them and to helpful behind-the-sceners Todd Phillips, Julie Johnson, Greg Zimprich, Lynne Galia, Mary Anne McAndrew, Geri Allen, Aettee Park,

Carole and Cevin Soling, Paul and Laurie Nardone, Thomas Wingham, John Greenleaf, George Krubert, Michael Krauss, Elaine Nadel, Kayla Nadel-LaMotta, Kim Rawlings, Susie Tofte, Leslie Richards, Marcia Snow, and especially E.G. Perry.

Thanks are also due recipe suppliers or testers Terri Fleming, Hayne Bayless, Kimberly Kreiensieck-Sewell, Paige Isbutt, Linda Mill, Linda Reilly, Carol Lydon, Lucy Mathers, Karol Gibbons, Kristin Reiff, Chaim Potter, Louise Simons, and Joan Leof; Linda Campanelli, for photos and a guided tour of some of the best chocolate chip cookie places in L.A.; and, for help with research, writing, or obtaining photos or permissions, "Young" Jim Wyman, Doug Wyman, Blossom Gica, Ellen Slack, Barry Garfinkel, Debra Morway, Paula Price, Rosemary Morrow, Mark Garfinkel, Davie Hinshaw, Carol O'Neill, the staff at the Lilly, Newbury College, and Restaurant School at Walnut Hill College libraries, Francesca Crozier-Fitzgerald, Jodi Bosin, and Nina Willbach. Chapter 4 appears to have driven Nina into a music career (hopefully not permanently, if there is to be any bright future for journalism).

I'm also indebted to the Countryman crew, including Lisa Sacks, Cheryl Redmond, and Vicky Vaughn Shea, and headed by Kermit Hummel, for editorial and design savvy and, in Kermit's case, the smarts to marry the editor of a fine chocolate chip cookie book that came before. May our collaboration be at least as popular as hers and the Zismans'. And thanks to the skillful work of James Gregorio, I will forevermore be able to afford to buy rather than make chocolate chip cookies whenever I am feeling lazy.

And lastly but most importantly are Phil, sweeter than any cookie; and Ruth, without whom there would be neither chocolate chip cookies nor chocolate chip cookie books.

Permissions and Credits continued from page 4

by Ben Fink), 106 (photo by Jim Lennon), 108 and 109 (photo by Alexandra Rowley); Scott Blackwell/Immaculate Baking: 13 bottom, 172–174; Blossom Gica: 14, 49, 128, 140, 142; p. 18: Original courtesy Carol Cavanagh; Originals courtesy Mary Alice Kirby: 22, 23 and 26 bottom; p. 30: Baker's is a registered trademark of Kraft Foods Inc.; General Mills Archives: 32, 41, 58; General Mills Marketing Inc.: 64, 153 recipe and photo. Betty Crocker, Gold Medal, and Cookie Crisp are registered trademarks of General Mills, Inc. Pillsbury, Bake-Off and the Doughboy are registered trademarks of the Pillsbury Co.; p. 37: Photo by Mark Garfinkel; pp. 38–39: Essay by Richmond Talbot; Debbi Fields Rose: 40, 47, 50 right, 66 middle, 120; Wally Amos: 42, 43 upper left, 45, 46; p. 43 lower right: Nationaal Archief, Den Haag, Rijksfotoarchief: Fotocollectie Algemeen Nederlands Fotopersbureau (ANEFO), 1945–1989 — negatiefstroken zwart/wit, nummer toegang 2.24.01.05, bestanddeelnummer 919-3036. Wikimedia Commons (p.d.); p. 47: Mrs. Fields is a registered trademark of Mrs. Fields' Brand Inc.; p. 50 left: Photo of Waikiki Food Pantry Express store blessing courtesy Sullivan Family of Companies; p. 51: David's Cookies; p. 52: Chester Higgins Jr./*New York Times*/Redux; p. 55: Grandma's is a registered trademark of Frito-Lay, Inc.; p. 57: Davie Hinshaw/*The Charlotte Observer*; p. 61: Pepperidge Farm, Inc.; pp. 62–63: Elaine Nadel, donations for aspiring entrepreneurs can be sent to the Richard Edmund LaMotta Foundation, P.O. Box 309, Mount Kisco, N.Y. 10549; Marcia Snow: 66 left (photo by Dana Edmunds); p. 66 right: Ron Hester; Linda Rawlings: 71 upper right, 72; p. 74: Pamela Weekes; p. 76: David Leite (photo by EvanJoseph.com); p. 79 top: Guittard Chocolate Company; p. 79 bottom: Calvin and Hobbes © 1993 Watterson. Distr. by Universal Uclick. Reprinted with permission. All rights reserved; p. 80 Scott Samet; p. 81: Ben & Jerry's Homemade, Inc.; p. 82: AP Photo/J. Scott Applewhite; p. 85 right: Lance Private Brands, Div. of Snyders Lance, Inc.; p. 87: recipe inspired by Cookie Cake Pie in *CakeSpy Presents Sweet Treats for a Sugar-Filled Life* by Jessie Oleson and on www.cakespy.com; Linda Campanelli: 89, 90; Toni M. "Bumzy" Young: 91 (photo by Roland Paris); p. 93: Kirk "Captain Cookie" Francis; p. 96: Barbara O'Neill/The Cookie Studio; p. 97: Derby-Pie is a registered trademark of Kern's Kitchen; Kir Jensen: 107 (photo by Antoinette Bruno of StarChefs), 111 photo (by Lisa Warninger) and recipe; Metropolitan Bakery: 110, 114 photo (Kyle Born) and recipe (James Barrett); p. 113: Ricki Krupp/Ricki's Cookie Corner; p. 115: Tiffany Taylor Chen; p. 117: Karen Larson; p. 125: recipe courtesy Claudia Fleming; p. 175: Angela Wiese for Ripon Chamber of Commerce; p. 177: Sesame Workshop; p. 178: "got milk? ad from the California Milk Processor Board and Goodby Silverstein & Partners (photo © Terry Heffernan); Lucy Mathers: 180, 182 photo and recipe; Cody Downard for Beaver Creek: 179, 181; p. 184: Recipe courtesy Paige Isbutt; p. 185: George Silk/Time Life Pictures/Getty Images; p. 186: Peanuts © Peanuts Worldwide LLC. Dist. by Universal Uclick. Reprinted with permission. All rights reserved; DoubleTree is a registered trademark of Hilton Hospitality, Inc.

Recipe Index

Note: Page references in *italics* indicate recipe photographs.

General Index

Note: Page references in *italics* indicate photographs.

G

H